Sanctuaries

The West Coast and Southwest

Sanctuaries

The West Coast and Southwest

A Guide to Lodgings in
Monasteries, Abbeys, and Retreats
of the United States

Marcia and Jack Kelly

Bell Tower · New York

A percentage of the royalties from this book will go to the Seva Foundation (8 N. San Pedro Road, San Rafael, CA 94903) to help fund its worldwide program of compassionate action.

Design by Iris Weinstein.

Drawings by Barry J. Schiff/G & H SOHO LTD. from photographs by Jack Kelly, and maps by G & H SOHO LTD.

Published by Bell Tower, an imprint of Harmony Books, a division of Crown Publishers, Inc., 201 East 50th Street, New York, New York 10022. Member of the Crown Publishing Group. Random House, Inc. New York, Toronto, London, Sydney, Auckland

Bell Tower and colophon are registered trademarks of Crown Publishers, Inc.

Manufactured in the United States of America

Library of Congress Cataloging-in-Publication Data

Kelly, Marcia.

Sanctuaries—the West Coast and Southwest; a guide to lodgings in monasteries, abbeys, and retreats of the United States / Marcia and Jack Kelly—1st ed.

Includes index.

1. Monasteries—Southwest, New—Guest accommodations—Directories.

2. Monasteries—Northwest, Pacific—Guest accommodations—

Directories. 3. Abbeys—Southwest, New—Directories. 4. Abbeys—

Northwest, Pacific—Directories. 5. Retreats—Southwest, New—

Directories. 6. Retreats—Northwest, Pacific—Directories.

I. Kelly, Jack, 1934–. II. Title.

BL2527.S68K45 1993

647.947301—dc20 92-1037 CIP

ISBN 0-517-88007-5

10 9 8 7 6 5 4 3 2 1

First Edition

In Honor of our Parents

Rose and Joe Kelly
Gladys and Ben Marcus

We share with you a wonderful meditation we learned at the Insight Meditation Society in Barre, Massachusetts. Its purpose is to increase loving-kindness in the world. You say it first for yourself; then think of someone you love while saying it silently; then repeat it again thinking of someone you like; someone you feel neutral toward; someone you don't like very much; and finally send it to everyone in the world;

May you be free of inner and outer danger.
May you be free of mental suffering.
May you be free of physical suffering.
May you be able to care for yourself with ease and joy.

Contents

CONTENTS

CONTENTS

Introduction

Like the monasteries, abbeys, and retreats we visited in the Northeast for our first *Sanctuaries,* these places in the West and Southwest seem a world apart from our daily lives. Places we can go for reflection, solitude, rest, and renewal.

There were many differences between the Southwest and West Coast places and those we visited in the East, and that was an added pleasure for two Easterners. Looking out at the world from a hermitage in the Arizona desert or from a snow-covered cabin at 8,500 feet in the mountains of New Mexico was awe-inspiring, and completely new, as was listening to the voices of Trappist monks singing the liturgy in Oregon, Zen Buddhists chanting in Northern California, or an evening of drumming on Salt Spring Island, British Columbia. We saw otters cross our path on the beach below one monastery, Orcas whales cavort beside our ferryboat on the way to another, and the first flight of a baby bald eagle from the lawn of an island retreat—a look at the natural world from a fresh perspective.

You'll notice that we strayed just over the border, once into Baja California and on three occasions into British Columbia. We couldn't resist.

In answer to questions often asked, we'll share some basics here that should prove useful in your travels:

Philosophy The places that have chosen a ministry of hospitality offer it with a spirit of openness and warmth, and unless noted in the text, welcome people of all faiths, with no requirement to attend any services or participate in any activities. You are free to join them in prayer or to just enjoy the surroundings, and no attempt will be made to urge you to do anything other than what you choose. We came as casual guests, for short visits, and our observations reflect this experience and not what it might be like as long-term residents.

Purpose Monasteries and abbeys are usually functioning religious communities that have some rooms for visitors, while the purpose of retreat houses is to provide a setting for groups to hold meetings or retreats. There are often rooms available for individuals (private retreatants) even when a group retreat is going on. Individuals can sometimes join in the group sessions, and can almost always join in prayer services. It is important to remember that the people who live in these places are not prepared to do psychological counseling, so don't make such a retreat if that is your expectation or need.

Settings and accommodations We stayed in everything from seaside estates with exquisite tropical gardens to simple cabins in the woods, reached only by a swaying suspension bridge. Accommodations ranged from a beautiful suite with private bath overlooking the sea to a simple room heated with only a woodstove, and an outhouse 70 yards down a snow-covered pathway.

Some places have hermitages, usually for one person who wants to be alone, sometimes for two. Although many of the buildings were once houses of the very rich, the accommodations are usually simple, though comfortable and clean. Most places welcome men, women, and children. Any variations are noted in the text. Where dormitory space is provided, it is separate for men and women in most cases. You should not bring pets with you, but you will encounter resident cats and dogs from time to time, as in the East. On this trip we also met resident llamas, peacocks, emus, and even a bobcat!

Costs There is an effort to keep the fees moderate, though in many cases they do not cover all the expenses, so supplemental donations are gratefully accepted. If the fee is a burden, special arrangements can be discussed. Many places have work/study programs; some have work/exchange available for a period of time. Prices for 1991–1992 range from $15 to $175 a night, often with reduced rates for longer stays. Fees usually include three meals a day, but it's important to confirm meal arrangements when making reservations. Some places have cooks only when a group is coming, so you may have to bring your own food or dine in the area.

Customs, comportment, attire It is a custom in this world to "turn the bed," or make the bed with fresh sheets for the next guest. Occasionally you may have to bring your own linens or sleeping bag, something you should confirm when making reservations. In some places, guests are expected to pitch in and help with chores (this is noted in the text); in others, the staff prefer no help at all. Work on the property, with the community, is usually available on request.

Courtesy and sensitivity to others is the general rule. Guests and community are there for quiet and contemplation, so radios, typewriters, and chatting in the hallways or chapel will only be disturbing. Following the lead of the community will easily carry you through any local customs.

Attire can be casual, though it should be respectful in those places that are religious communities. In this book we've included some hot springs and other nonreligious retreats. These are extremely informal in every way. Many residents of the religious communities wear work shirts and jeans except when in chapel, though guests may dress casually even there. We certainly didn't identify the man in overalls and a knitted cap leaning against the barn as a swami when we approached one center in California.

Reservations Reservations are essential. Some places are booked weeks or months ahead on weekends, particularly for groups. Individuals can often get a bed with less notice and weekdays are easier for all. In any case, do not appear without having called ahead, and if you can't come, be sure to give as much notice as possible, or if it's at the last minute, offer to forfeit the fee, since these places depend on the income to survive.

Transportation To help orient you geographically, we have included driving directions, but some places are very hard to find, so be prepared for wrong turns. In snowy places chains and sand are good added precautions. Most places have directions in their brochures for arrival by car or public transportation. Many can arrange to meet you at the airport or station.

What to bring It's a good idea to bring a flashlight to find your way at night, on walks, down the hall to the bathroom, or down the path to the outhouse! We stayed in two places that not only had flashlights but umbrellas in every room, but that is rare. Be prepared with extra sweaters in cold weather, cool clothes in the summer. Often there's a place to swim on the property or nearby, so pack bathing suits for those places that require them. Be sure to ask if you need to bring any food or linens.

Day visits Many of the places are available for individuals or groups for day use.

Access for the handicapped Be sure to inquire ahead. Some places are completely equipped, and others are still in the process of making everything accessible.

Other places At the end of each section, there is a list of additional places that were recommended to us but that we have not yet visited.

Conclusion Many people ask why someone would want to visit a monastery, abbey, or retreat. Our answer can be based only on what we've found in over 200 visits, and which we've tried to reflect in each essay in each book. Not only is this an opportunity for a time apart (some say they feel a sense of peacefulness as they enter the gates) but a time to reach for our best selves, to think about and practice our best values on a daily basis, then take them back to our "regular" lives.

We share this "turning the bed" prayer, found at one of our stops, with special thanks to all who shared their favorite places with us:

Dear Friend,
    As I made this bed, I offered a prayer for whoever would sleep in it next.
I prayed for your rest and a sense of peace; for the refreshment of your body and the renewal of your spirit.
    I prayed that God would bless you with love, give you a sense of His presence, and comfort you with mercy and grace.
    I prayed trusting in God's love which can bind us all together.

Marcia and Jack Kelly
NEW YORK CITY

Sanctuaries

The West Coast and Southwest

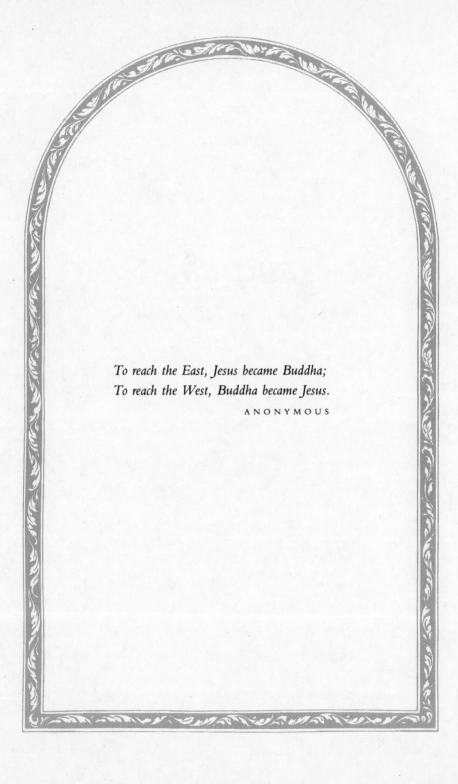

To reach the East, Jesus became Buddha;
To reach the West, Buddha became Jesus.

ANONYMOUS

Arizona

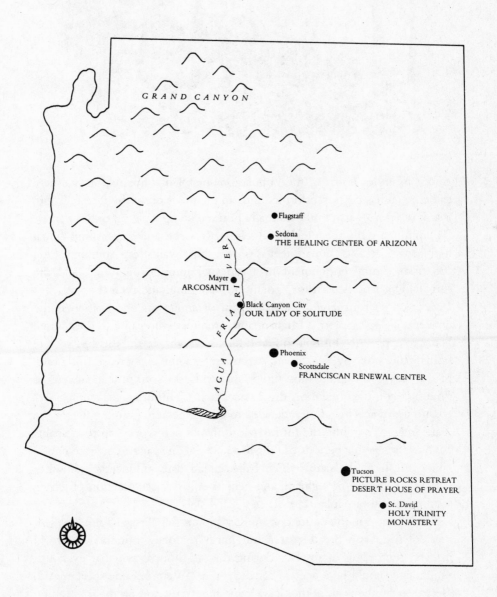

GRAND CANYON

● Flagstaff

● Sedona
THE HEALING CENTER OF ARIZONA

Mayer ●
ARCOSANTI

● Black Canyon City
OUR LADY OF SOLITUDE

● Phoenix

● Scottsdale
FRANCISCAN RENEWAL CENTER

● Tucson
PICTURE ROCKS RETREAT
DESERT HOUSE OF PRAYER

● St. David
HOLY TRINITY
MONASTERY

A G U A   F R I A   R I V E R

Arcosanti
Mayer, AZ

About 65 miles north of the population sprawl of Phoenix, an 860-acre cattle ranch has been transformed into an urban vision of the future. There is a development that will eventually house 6,000 people on only 17 acres. By eliminating the automobile, which needs streets and garages, individual living space of 2,000 square feet is only a short walk from anything. One can find cultural enrichment in a series of interlocking units, and the surrounding land is used for agriculture, ranching, and recreation.

Arcosanti (from *arcology,* an amalgam of *architecture* and *ecology*) is the concept of Paolo Soleri, an Italian-born architect who came to the United States to apprentice himself to Frank Lloyd Wright. In the early 1970s, the brilliant and controversial Soleri, described by some as a daydreaming utopian and by others as the most important architect of our time, believed the time had come to make his dream a reality. Committed to keeping Arcosanti mortgage-free, Soleri decided to charge helpers a modest fee for the experience of building the future. More than 3,000 workshop participants have lived here for periods of four to six weeks in spartan concrete cubes, taking meals in the café, which bakes bread daily. Concerts and other cultural events are brought in, and helpers enjoy the interaction of fellow workers and the regular staff of 50.

Once a month, the entire community gathers for "Frugal Soup," a plain meal of soup and bread, water and juice, to focus thoughts on world hunger, reminding themselves during this 1½-hour event that even this simple fare would be a feast to some people. "We are," one speaker said, "like fleas on the back of the tiger, living in a flea world on the frightening tiger of reality."

The buildings of Arcosanti are on a mesa above the Agua Fria River valley, a few miles from Route 17—the major road between Flagstaff and Phoenix. The building outlines can be seen from the highway. It appears like a space village on the planet desert. There are 10 guest rooms for 17 people. Visitors are welcome to retreat here to view the future.

More than $3 million has been spent so far, with funds earned from the sale of bronze and ceramic wind bells. Slowly but surely the vision grows to reality through the dedicated efforts of staff and workshop members. In the main office, there is a model of the completed Arcosanti. Soleri was once asked how much it would cost to complete the entire project. Reportedly, he smiled and answered: "About the price of one attack bomber."

Arcosanti
HC74, Box 4136
Mayer, AZ 86333
(602) 632-7135

Accommodations: *10 rooms for 17 men, women, and children; café and bakery open daily with organic vegetarian meals available, and delicious home-baked breads and sweets, all moderately priced; "Frugal Soup," a once-a-month 1½-hour ritual instituted by Paolo Soleri to focus on world hunger; 5-week workshops; special concerts, lectures, other events throughout year; Elderhostels; 860 acres with Indian artifacts; swimming pool; open year-round except Thanksgiving and Christmas; $15–$25 a day room cost, 2-bedroom penthouse "Sky Suite" $50 a day.*

Directions: *Rte. 17 to Exit 262 (Cordes Junction Rd.) and follow signs for Arcosanti (2½ miles on dirt road).*

Desert House of Prayer
Tucson, AZ

The Desert House of Prayer in the Sonoran Desert is a place where "in a climate of quiet and solitude, with the support of a small community of people committed to the contemplative life, one might come for a time to renew and deepen one's relationship with God . . . where one can get more deeply rooted and centered in God through prayer." This is the mission statement of Father John Kane and two sisters who began in a building at Picture Rocks Retreat (see page 14), and eventually acquired 31 acres just across the road, where they established this haven for solitude and quiet prayer.

The current staff of five has 12 rooms with private baths available for retreatants. Three meals a day are provided in the dining room; breakfast and lunch are picked up there and eaten in silence. At the evening meal, which is taken with the community, talking is permitted. There are two self-contained hermitages nearby, well thought out and beautifully crafted. The mighty saguaro cacti, some standing 40 feet high, seem to guard against intrusion.

In the chapel, a separate building with a picture window at one end framing a magnificent desert scene, the community meets three times a day for mass, a prayer service, and 1½ hours of meditation that is similar to Zen sitting and is broken by walking meditation at 25-minute intervals; each person sits forward in the chair, spine erect, synchronizing the repetition of a mantra with the breath.

There is a library with 6,000 volumes and hundreds of tapes, including a complete set of Thomas Merton's discussions and addresses, many of which he made when he was novice master at Gethsemani.

The outdoor stations of the cross were donated by Dr. Richard Chun of Honolulu. The scenes on wooden crosses are complemented by the desert chaparral and the rugged mountain background. As one retreatant remarked: "The grace of the place is its silence."

Desert House of Prayer
7350 W. Picture Rocks Rd.
Tucson, AZ 85743
Mailing address: Box 574, Cortaro, AZ 85652
(602) 744-3825

Accommodations: For men and women, 12 rooms with private bath and 2 beautiful self-contained hermitages; studio for art projects under direction of community member who is an artist; breakfast and lunch in silence; Friday is a mitigated fast and silence all day; 1½ hours of daily prayer at morning praise, liturgy, and vespers; 4 hours daily serious reading, reflection, prayer, contemplation; Saturday night vigil until Sunday A.M. in 1-hour intervals; 31 acres of primitive high desert land at foot of Safford Peak in Tucson Mountains; monthly 3-day retreat with 6 hours daily of centering prayer; 6,000-book library; Wednesday night Peace & Justice Forum led by Father Ricardo Elford, a community member known for his sanctuary movement work; open year-round; $27 a day for first 3 days, $24 a day for extended stays; special rates for 3 months or more.

Directions: From Scottsdale/Phoenix take I-10 to Ina Rd. (Exit 248). Turn right on Ina Rd. for 3½ miles to Wade Rd. Left on Wade for 1 mile to entrance drive on right (watch for Picture Rocks Retreat sign on left—Desert House of Prayer is the second drive on right beyond that).

Franciscan Renewal Center
Scottsdale, AZ

Located between the mountains called Camelback and Mummy, the original buildings were constructed in 1945 as a resort. The Franciscans purchased the property in 1951 for use as a retreat center following the suggestion of the bishop of Tucson. The Spanish-style white-walled buildings with red-tile roofs were renamed Casa de Paz y Bien (House of Peace and Blessing) and the first retreats were held that year.

The facilities have been gradually expanded so that now there are comfortable rooms for 110 in several different buildings. All rooms have private baths with individual heat and air-conditioning. Meals are prepared by a professional staff and taken in the centrally located dining room. The campuslike complex still has the aura of a resort with beautiful lawns in courtyard settings, palm trees, and carefully tended flowering bushes. The desert and mountains make up the backdrop of this lush setting in Arizona's Valley of the Sun.

In 1970, the name was changed to Franciscan Renewal Center to emphasize the enlarged scope of the programs. While one department serves as a retreat haven and welcomes individuals and group meetings, the main thrust of the other division is to renew the spirit with adult education classes dealing with such diverse topics as self-healing, stress management, Bible studies, inner dance, and yoga. There are also programs on family unity and affirming positive family interaction, marriage counseling, and the 12-step series.

There is a restful, quiet chapel, which is large enough for 280 people and is the focal point of the center's activities. Though the center is Catholic-oriented, people of all denominations are encouraged to come and are welcomed in the spirit of St. Francis's prayer, which is displayed in large copper letters on a wall near the main entrance: "Where there is hatred, let me sow love; where there is injury, pardon; where there is doubt, faith."

Franciscan Renewal Center
5802 E. Lincoln Dr.
Scottsdale, AZ 85253
(602) 948-7460

Accommodations: *110 beds in comfortable singles, doubles, and triples with private baths for men, women, and children; buffet meals in dining room that will seat 160 at round tables; 10 conference rooms; mass daily; meditation chapel; 24 acres including Brother Mario's vegetable farm and orange, grapefruit, and lemon trees; Jacuzzi, large pool, volleyball, putting greens, on-campus walks and desert hikes, Mummy Mountain and Camelback Mountain hiking trails; open year-round; $45 for first night, $35 thereafter.*

Directions: *From I-17 North take Glendale Rd. exit. Follow Glendale Rd. right (east) 10 miles (it becomes Lincoln). Watch for 4-way intersection at Tatum. Continue straight on E. Lincoln 2 more miles and watch for center on left.*

The Healing Center of Arizona
Sedona, AZ

South of Flagstaff, where the red rock buttes of Arizona flow into canyons, the town of Sedona sits in the rugged foothills of the Rocky Mountains. Native Americans have been coming here for centuries to be refreshed and healed, for this place is said to be the site of an energy vortex. This has long been recognized by those with psychic powers who have settled here and given the town the reputation, though it has no TV station, of being the home of 400 channels.

Native Sedonan John Paul Weber returned after ten years in San Francisco to found the Healing Center of Arizona. Choosing a site in Wilson Canyon, where juniper trees grow in abundance, he meditated on a rocky outcrop as to what kind of building to construct. His meditations inspired him to build a large geodesic dome surrounded by four smaller ones. With the help of clients and friends, construction began in 1981 and was completed five years later. When the structure had been framed, before the doors and windows were installed, John Paul was working inside one day when he heard a loud crash. He discovered that the boulder on which he had spent so much time meditating had broken loose from the cliff, rolled through a door opening, and come to rest in the corner of a room. As big as a table, it still remains there, obviously wanting not to be left out.

There are 4,200 square feet in the five domes, shaped like a large daisy, where up to 20 people can be accommodated, some in private rooms. Glorious flowering plants thrive in the light, airy space, which is tastefully furnished. The bathrooms are tiled and gleaming, and there are a hot tub, a sauna, and a flotation tank; one of the smaller domes is a meditation chamber, where energy seems amplified and awareness increased. Delicious food—usually vegetarian—is served in the main living-dining space. There are superb views across the canyon where the magnificent rocks are outlined in the normally blue sky.

The center offers personalized retreats tailored to the needs of individuals. Some involve massage and acupressure, along with the use of heat and water. There are hiking trails into the canyon, and the awesome beauty and clear air of the Arizona landscape help one relax and let go of any illness. This place seems to be a major step toward what John Paul describes as "the need for centers of light and love of all humanity that are nondenominational and open to all to give grounding and remembrance of the divine presence."

The Healing Center of Arizona
25 Wilson Canyon Rd.
Sedona, AZ 86336
(602) 282-7710

Accommodations: Men, women, and children can be accommodated in 3 lovely doubles with queen-size beds, and a dorm room with futons can be used for larger groups; 2 individual dome shelters for those wishing to be alone; "earthship" (house made of tires) being constructed in the hillside for another quiet sanctuary; tiled baths filled with plants and fountains; delicious, home-cooked food can be provided if requested; meditation room, flotation tank, sauna, sweat lodge, medicine wheel, t'ai chi ch'uan, hot tub; many therapies available; open year-round; $50–$65 a day for room; holistic or healing retreats $140 a day; weekly rates available.

Directions: Rte. 89A, a beautiful mountain canyon road to Sedona from Flagstaff. Turn right on Jordan Rd. to Hillside Dr., then right 1 block to Mountain View and left to Wilson Canyon Rd. and right to dome at end. Little neighborhood roads, so watch carefully for signs.

Holy Trinity Monastery
St. David, AZ

Deep in Apache territory, about 14 miles north of Tombstone and 17 miles from Cochise Stronghold, this Benedictine monastery was founded seren-dipitously. Formerly the Wilderness Ranch for Boys, the 93 acres was run by an ecumenical group to help young men in trouble. While giving a retreat in Tucson, Father Louis Hassenfus of the Pecos Benedictine Mon-astery (see page 140) was asked to take over the ranch in order to provide a spiritual renewal center for the whole area. Wary of committing himself to such a venture and concerned about what would happen to his oblate outreach program, he agreed on condition that the Pecos group gave consensus approval. Knowing that they could never reach consensus on anything, he felt certain that his ministerial direction would not change. Much to his surprise, there was a unanimous vote that it should be done, and in September 1974, accompanied by two helpers, he founded Holy Trinity Monastery.

Following the liberal tradition of Pecos, and the evolving growth and modifications to monastic traditions, Holy Trinity is a community com-posed of priests and brothers, sisters, lay people, and married couples. The regular community of nine monks, six sisters, and six lay people work at separate responsibilities such as tending the orchards, cooking and cleaning for the regular visitors and retreatants, running the gift shop and art gallery, and maintaining the grounds and caring for the variety of farm animals and the peacocks.

Thousands of people have come here to experience the monastic space. Some couples come regularly, for months at a time, and hook up their homes on wheels to power and water in a back section, and join the community in work and prayer. "It's uncanny," one monk said, "how people come along with skills to help solve some problem or help with building, as needed."

The monastery's income comes from varied sources, including the sale of pecans from the 150-tree orchard and the spring and autumn festivals, which grow each year in popularity and participation. In 1990, there were 65 booths rented to craftspeople who sold to the large crowds attracted by the great food and music provided by friends and oblates.

Visitors are expected to observe the monastic disciplines of silence, solitude, and prayer. There are six private rooms with shared baths for guests in the Casa de Bernardo, which has a comfortable lounge with coffee, tea, and snacks. Meals are taken family-style with the community in the main dining room a short distance across the courtyard. Prayer services are held daily in the beautiful adobe chapel with mass celebrated at noon. A nearby pond is home to many ducks. The striking outdoor stations of the cross, behind the chapel, are made from weathered wood and old ranch implements.

Unnecessary talk should be avoided, remembering, as one monk said: "The Lord has a sense of humor, and the Holy Spirit's got this ground, so just be still and you'll get the answers."

Holy Trinity Monastery
P.O. Box 298
St. David, AZ 85630
(602) 720-4642

Accommodations: *6 comfortable, well-kept double rooms for men and women in the guesthouse (with more planned); 16 RV hookups for short-term visitors; guests and community share refectory meals; mass daily plus 4 prayer times in lovely chapel; Friday "Taizé" 7:30–8:30 P.M. for peace; unique stations of the cross; lots of work available—on farm, household, repairs, office; 17-mile walk on dirt road to mountains; library, bookstore, art gallery, museum; open year-round; suggested donation for 1–7-day private retreats: $22.50 a day; group rates available.*

Directions: *From Tucson take Arizona Rte. 10 for 45 miles to Benson (Exit 303). Follow U.S. 80 South 9 miles to St. David. Monastery is on west side of road. 2 miles south of St. David watch for large white cross and* HOLY TRINITY MONASTERY *sign at gate.*

Our Lady of Solitude
House of Prayer
Black Canyon City, AZ

Up a long, steep drive to a mesa in the Sonoran Desert, this house-of-prayer complex sits alone and quiet. It's hard to imagine a more fitting place for solitude and contemplative prayer. The road to Phoenix can be seen to the north, but traffic noise is nonexistent and views to Black Canyon City and the mountains beyond accentuate the separation.

Through a joint effort of a Mexican layman seeking spiritual fulfillment and the Catholic bishop of Phoenix, who sought to establish a contemplative group in the diocese, benefactors funded a house of prayer in 1980. Four years later a donation made it possible for the prayer community to buy these 20 acres surrounded by state and federal land. At the end of the drive, the main house sits on a high point with sweeping desert views to the south and west. There are six private guest rooms with shared baths in the house, which has a spacious reading room stocked with more than 1,400 books; meals are taken in the adjacent dining room.

On a separate knoll is the Dwelling Place, a chapel dedicated in 1988. The circular stucco building has a picture window looking out over the valley below; a window-cross of stained glass depicting Christ in a collage of color is the only decoration in the subdued interior.

Near the chapel are four sturdy and comfortable hermitages set apart from one another. Each hermitage has a kitchenette, a single bedroom, a private bath, and cooling and heating units. The absolute privacy enables retreatants to appreciate the silence and sweetness of the surrounding desert air.

Signs on the property advise NO HUNTING EXCEPT FOR PEACE AND GOD and NO SMOKING EXCEPT FOR THE FIRE OF PRAYER.

Our Lady of Solitude House of Prayer
P.O. Box 1140
Black Canyon City, AZ 85324
(602) 374-9204

Accommodations: *4 private hermitages (18 × 18) with bath, kitchenette, porch, for men and women, located on desert mesa overlooking mountains, and 6 private rooms in main house (you are encouraged to bring your own sheets and towels if driving); for hermitage meals bring simple food since a toaster oven, small refrigerator, and 1 burner are available; 3 meals provided in main house; daily communion services at meditation chapel, the Dwelling Place, and sung Vespers on Sunday (evensong); all is in total silence here; library open 9 A.M.–noon daily; miles of desert to walk (bring sturdy shoes and hat); 1-day–3-week private or directed retreats, 2–4-week desert spirituality live-ins; 2-month–12-month sabbatical live-ins; open year-round; suggested donation: $25 a night; reservations needed at least 2 weeks in advance.*

Directions: *Take I-17 North from Phoenix to Exit 242; go to far right (Frontage Rd.) and turn right at first dirt road (marked by tall transformer); drive up the hill (past KOA on left) in low gear; total distance from exit to Our Lady of Solitude is 1 mile.*

Picture Rocks Retreat
Tucson, AZ

In the foothills of the Tucson Mountains, at the edge of Saguaro National Monument–West, sit the 75 acres of Picture Rocks Retreat, named after the petroglyphs carved long ago by Hohokam Indians on rocks jutting up on the property, only a few minutes' walk from the parking area. The giant saguaro cacti, standing like sentinels, add charm and mystery. In the early evening, the magical colors of the desert sky are incredibly beautiful.

In the early 1960s, the bishop of Tucson invited the Redemptorist priests to found a retreat haven. The story goes that one of those priests planted medals of St. Girard on this property asking for help to obtain it, and it worked. The Redemptorists follow the direction of their founder, St. Alphonsus de Mary Liguori, to do extraordinary preaching. They believe that the desert reminds us that to survive we must adapt, just as plants and animals adapt to the most unsupportive conditions. During a retreat in the desert, the analogy of adaptation to one's personal world becomes easier to understand.

There are comfortable, motel-like rooms for 83, some with private bath, in low-slung buildings a short distance from the dining room/cafeteria, where three meals a day are served. The stone chapel was constructed from rock quarried nearby. A visiting Irish stonemason built the entire chapel almost single-handedly. There are outdoor stations of the cross deliberately canted to give different views of the desert. The nearby Saguaro National Monument provides miles of hiking trails.

The community of priests, sisters, and lay people who live here offers a full schedule of retreats and a wide variety of programs for single women, senior citizens, overeaters, Knights of Columbus, and Lutheran ministers, among many others. There are courses using art as meditation and one that examines "Spirituality for the Twenty-first Century."

Private retreatants are welcome at any time. The community and staff come together for prayer in the chapel daily and visitors may attend.

Picture Rocks Retreat
7101 W. Picture Rocks Rd.
Tucson, AZ 85743
(602) 744-3400

Accommodations: *83 beds in singles and doubles for men and women in comfortable motel-style rooms; tasty homemade meals served cafeteria-style in pleasant dining room with desert view and lots of bird life outside windows; Eucharist and community prayer services daily; 75 acres of cactus-covered desert at foot of Tucson Mountains with miles of hills and trails; Picture Rock petroglyphs on property, at edge of Saguaro National Monument; open year-round; write for schedule and current rates for private or group retreatants.*

Directions: *From the intersection of I-10 and Ina Rd. (Exit 248), cross I-10 going west on Ina Rd.; go 3½ miles to Wade Rd., then turn left onto Wade for 1 mile to center on left.*

Arizona: Other Places

Mount Claret Cursillo Center, 4633 N. 54th St., **Phoenix,** AZ 85018. (602) 955-7890

Servants of Christ Monastery, 6533 N. 39th Ave., **Phoenix,** AZ 85019. (602) 841-8634

Arizona Church Conference Center, P.O. Box 1986, **Prescott,** AZ 86302. (602) 445-3499

Prescott Pines Baptist Camp, P.O. Box 1226, **Prescott,** AZ 86302. (602) 445-5225

The Rim Institute, 6835 Pepper Treat Ln., **Scottsdale,** AZ 85253. (602) 263-0551 and 478-4727

St. Rita Abbey, HC1 Box 929, **Sonoita,** AZ 85637. (602) 455-5595

Madonna House/La Casa de Nuestra Señora, 213 Jefferson, **Winslow,** AZ 86047. (602) 289-3007

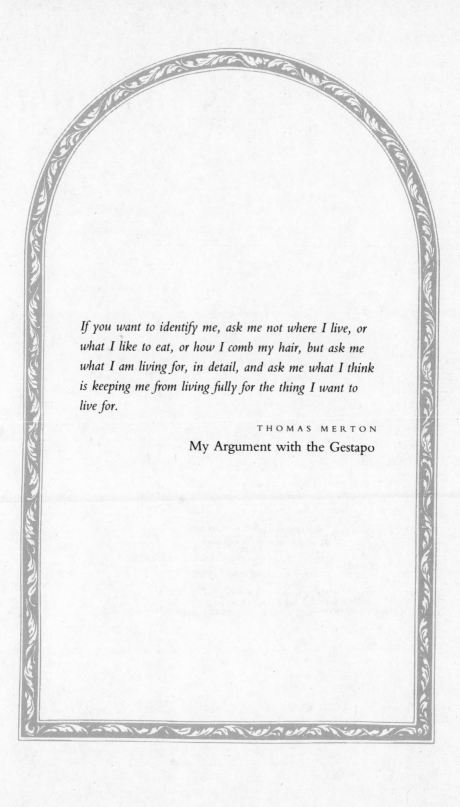

*If you want to identify me, ask me not where I live, or
what I like to eat, or how I comb my hair, but ask me
what I am living for, in detail, and ask me what I think
is keeping me from living fully for the thing I want to
live for.*

THOMAS MERTON
My Argument with the Gestapo

California

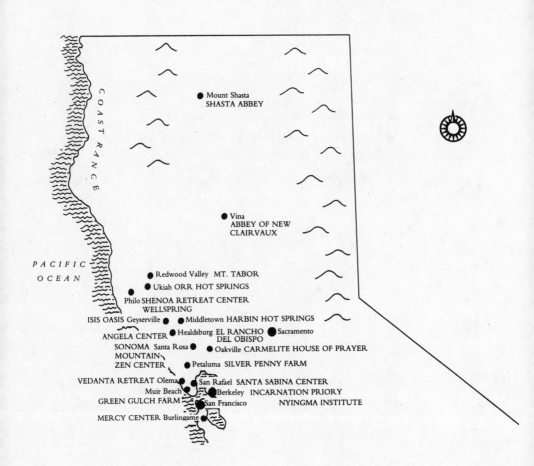

COAST RANGE

PACIFIC
OCEAN

● Mount Shasta
SHASTA ABBEY

● Vina
ABBEY OF NEW
CLAIRVAUX

● Redwood Valley MT. TABOR
● Ukiah ORR HOT SPRINGS
Philo SHENOA RETREAT CENTER
WELLSPRING
ISIS OASIS Geyserville ● ● Middletown HARBIN HOT SPRINGS
ANGELA CENTER ● Healdsburg EL RANCHO ● Sacramento
DEL OBISPO
SONOMA Santa Rosa ● ● Oakville CARMELITE HOUSE OF PRAYER
MOUNTAIN
ZEN CENTER ● Petaluma SILVER PENNY FARM
VEDANTA RETREAT Olema ● ● San Rafael SANTA SABINA CENTER
Muir Beach ● Berkeley INCARNATION PRIORY
GREEN GULCH FARM ● San Francisco NYINGMA INSTITUTE
MERCY CENTER Burlingame ●

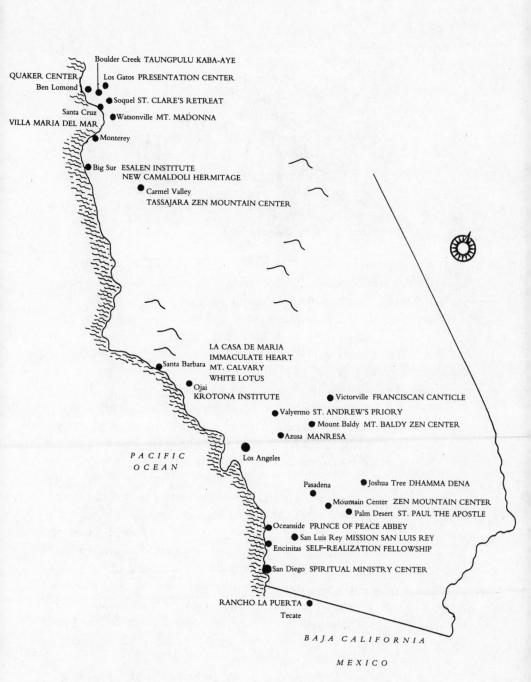

Boulder Creek TAUNGPULU KABA-AYE
Los Gatos PRESENTATION CENTER
QUAKER CENTER
Ben Lomond
Soquel ST. CLARE'S RETREAT
Santa Cruz
VILLA MARIA DEL MAR
Watsonville MT. MADONNA
Monterey

Big Sur ESALEN INSTITUTE
NEW CAMALDOLI HERMITAGE
Carmel Valley
TASSAJARA ZEN MOUNTAIN CENTER

LA CASA DE MARIA
IMMACULATE HEART
Santa Barbara MT. CALVARY
WHITE LOTUS
Ojai
KROTONA INSTITUTE
Victorville FRANCISCAN CANTICLE
Valyermo ST. ANDREW'S PRIORY
Mount Baldy MT. BALDY ZEN CENTER
Azusa MANRESA

PACIFIC
OCEAN
Los Angeles

Pasadena
Joshua Tree DHAMMA DENA
Mountain Center ZEN MOUNTAIN CENTER
Palm Desert ST. PAUL THE APOSTLE
Oceanside PRINCE OF PEACE ABBEY
San Luis Rey MISSION SAN LUIS REY
Encinitas SELF-REALIZATION FELLOWSHIP
San Diego SPIRITUAL MINISTRY CENTER

RANCHO LA PUERTA
Tecate

BAJA CALIFORNIA

MEXICO

Abbey of New Clairvaux
Vina, CA

In 1955 in the orchard belt of Tehama County, part of the rich farming region in the northern Sacramento Valley, Trappist monks from Gethsemani, Kentucky, acquired about 600 fertile acres. Over the years, they have transformed much of the land into prune and walnut orchards. The trees grow in long, orderly rows as far as the eye can see. The prunes are sold to Sunsweet, the walnuts to Diamond, and the income from the harvest supports the monastery.

Named after the Abbey of Clairvaux in France, where St. Bernard founded the Cistercian order in 1115, New Clairvaux ("clear valley" or "valley of light") was once a winery when Leland Stanford owned the property. The large brick building to the right of the monastic enclosure, now used for equipment storage, was once the largest winery in the country.

More than 30 monks live here and are summoned six times a day by the bells to the chapel to sing the canonical hours. Guests and visitors are welcome at all services. After Compline at 7:30 P.M., Grand Silence is observed till morning. There are single and double rooms with private baths for guests in an unobtrusive motel-like building and in two other buildings. The rooms are comfortable and well maintained. A guest refectory is in a separate building; good meals are brought from the monastery kitchen and served family-style. There is a separate room off the main dining area for those who are observing silence. Guests clean up after the meals. Coffee, tea, and snacks are always available here.

There are no formal retreats but, as one monk observed, "True hospitality is giving someone the space to breathe. If you want to talk to a monk, you'll have to ask."

There is a separate chapel for prayer and meditation just behind the main entrance reception area. A pleasant building with a fountain in front, it has a timeless look and recalls the words of Thomas Merton: "Actually, what matters about the monastery is precisely that it is radically different from the world. The apparent 'pointlessness' of the monastery in the eyes of the world is exactly what gives it a real reason for existing. In a world of noise, confusion, and conflict it is necessary that there be a place of silence, inner discipline, and peace."

Deer Creek winds around the property and flows into the Sacramento River. There is fine walking along the creek and, during the evening, on the service roads through the orchards. "It gets so quiet here at night," one guest observed, "you can hear a prune drop."

Abbey of New Clairvaux
Seventh and C Sts.
Vina, CA 96092
(916) 839-2434 Guestmaster

Accommodations: *For men and women, 6 singles and 2 doubles with 2 suites in new wing with private baths, and 10 rooms in old buildings with 1 suite and private bath; umbrella and flashlight in each room; tasty vegetarian meals in guest refectory, with homemade bread, jellies, home-grown fruits in syrup (pears, prunes), pick-up breakfast, main meal at noon and supper left on buffet for guests to serve themselves; Vigils, Lauds, Terce, mass, Sext, None, Vespers, Compline daily, announced by ringing bell; 15,000 walnut and prune trees on 600 acres; 1²⁄₁₀-mile walk one-way to Sacramento River at end of orchards; closed last 2 weeks of August annually for prune harvest; suggested minimum donation: $20 a day; 3-day stay requested.*

Directions: *Rte. I-5 to Corning, South Ave. exit. Follow South Ave. 9 miles east over 1 set of railroad tracks, Sacramento River; after second set of tracks take an immediate left on Rowles Rd. into Vina. Go to Seventh St. and take left to C St. and monastery.*

Angela Center
Santa Rosa, CA

The large, handsome building of the Angela Center was built in 1964 as a novitiate house for the Catholic Ursulan order of sisters. Since the mid-1970s, the center has been involved in retreat and education programs. The 60 acres of woods and fields around the center—some rented for sheep grazing—sit up from the Old Redwood Highway just north of Santa Rosa. The center is named after Angela Merici, the sixteenth-century founder of the Ursulines, who welcomed women of all ages and backgrounds to live an expression of their faith, according to the needs of the time.

The Ursulines are traditional educators (originally of young girls), and at the Angela Center they offer a series of programs that seek to integrate spirituality, psychology, social responsibility, and the arts. The courses, which usually meet one evening a week, include journal keeping, the Enneagram, and prayer as therapy; in 1991 there was even an examination of James Joyce's *Ulysses* as an odyssey of humanity's everlasting search for home. There are one-day and weekend retreats; some are thematic and relate to a particular season of the year.

Though Catholic in tradition, the center is very ecumenical and is open to all who believe they have something to share with the entire human family. "We are all heading for the same place," one sister said, "though our approaches may be different. Our spiritual and psychological grounding is in the timeless stories that underlie all religions and assure us that our struggles are part of a larger experience."

The center has 102 beds in clean, neat rooms with shared bathrooms. There is a high-ceilinged chapel with wood-paneled walls, the windows set above eye level so that attention is kept within. Comfortable chairs can be moved about the carpeted floor. The plain white altar table sits before a black-tiled back wall where an unadorned crucifix is dimly lighted. In a hallway near the chapel is a beautifully carved wooden crucifixion scene. There is also an inviting inner courtyard. Behind the center, one can walk up into the fields and woods.

Angela Center
535 Angela Dr.
Santa Rosa, CA 95401
(707) 528-8578

Accommodations: *48 beds in twin rooms and 54 beds in triples for men and women; buffet-style meals; services with program or at convent on property daily; very ecumenical—"We share things in common with the whole human family"; 60 acres of rolling hills with sheep, farms, lake; courtyard with orange, grapefruit, lemon trees; open year-round; $94 a weekend.*

Directions: *Hwy. 101 to Santa Rosa, Mendocino exit, and follow Old Redwood Hwy. 1 mile to* ANGELA CENTER *sign and Angela Dr. on right.*

Carmelite House of Prayer
Oakville, CA

In the lush Napa Valley, where every available plot of earth is planted with vineyards, St. Helena, Rutherford, and Oakville are little towns along the road where the great local wineries produce some of the finest California wine. About a mile from Route 29, set on a knoll almost hidden from sight by tall trees, the former Doak Mansion was acquired by the Catholic Discalced Carmelite friars in 1955. The three-story Georgian-style brick building had been unused for 15 years and was "a melancholy relic of former glory sleeping peacefully in lonely splendor amid the trees," as one historian described it. Since then, the Carmelites have restored the mansion and grounds, adding a chapel at one end of the building and reclaiming the large circular fountain on the back lawn. Some of the original grapevine cuttings were supplied in the 1850s by priests from the California missions, so it seems fitting that priests live here now, providing some measure of spirituality in this extremely commercial region—perhaps doubly fitting once you realize that the word *Carmel* is derived from the Hebrew *kerem-el,* which means "vineyard of the Lord."

There is a community here of five priests who have about 16 beds available for guests—some on the second and third floors of the mansion and others in a cottage at the edge of the vineyards. Breakfast and lunch are self-service but dinner is with the community in the dining room. There are morning and late-afternoon prayer services where guests are welcome.

Private retreatants can be accommodated. There are regular "poustinia" weekends, which have no structure, techniques, methods, or rules, but provide a time for solitude, silence, prayer, meditation, and fasting as a way to search for God and self. These weekends were described by one of the priests in this way: *Dolce far niente, e dopo reposare* ("It is sweet to do nothing, and relax afterward"). After a weekend here one S & L executive with marital problems and a job in jeopardy said to a priest, "I don't know why people aren't knocking your doors down. . . . There are a lot of them out there like me."

Carmelite House of Prayer
Oakville Grade Rd.
Oakville, CA 94562
(707) 944-2454

Accommodations: *Accommodations for 16 men and women in 6-bedroom cottage with kitchen, living room, and 3 bedrooms through one entrance and 3 bedrooms through the other entrance, plus 8 rooms with double beds in main house and 2 rooms on the second floor; pick-up breakfast and lunch in stocked kitchens and home-cooked dinner with community; morning prayer, midday prayer, and mass, 5 P.M. office, evening prayer; walking on beautiful 30-acre grounds with adjoining vineyards; 2 benefits yearly, a wine auction in spring and a barbecue dinner in September; open year-round; $30 a day, 2-day minimum; $25 a day, 5-day retreat.*

Directions: *Rte. 29 to Oakville (in the Napa Valley), 3 miles north of Yountville, turn left on Oakville Grade Rd. and watch for sign on right approximately 1 mile.*

Dhamma Dena
Joshua Tree, CA

On Copper Mountain Mesa, in the California high desert just north of Joshua Tree National Monument, Buddhist teacher Ruth Denison purchased 12½ acres of land in 1978. Having camped in the area for years, she loved the isolation and quiet where she and her family and friends could get away for rest and repair. Ruth initially intended to use the spot as a private sanctuary but she often invited her students to spend time there and eventually she began to hold retreats. In the 1980s, a community began to form and facilities were added. A meditation hall, big enough for 50 people or more, was built a short distance from the main house. Here the community gathers for Vipassana (insight) meditation with helpful comments from Ruth voiced to the meditators during the sittings: "Watch your breathing . . . become your breathing . . . sink into the silence of your breathing."

There are formal retreats in Vipassana held periodically; private retreatants can usually be accommodated any time. Men and women stay in separate housing. The accommodations are spartan and visitors should bring sleeping bags and be prepared to use an outhouse. Light vegetarian meals are served in the main house. Water is trucked in and is treated as precious; every drop is saved to water plants. The runoff from the shower house is captured and used to refresh the oleanders and pampa grass.

A youthful and vigorous ambience permeates this isolated desert setting where creosote bushes grow in abundance. The tall, spindly plants survive by joining their roots, a marvel of adaptation, suggesting the analogy of like-minded people surviving and growing by joining their spiritual roots. Awareness is heightened in the desert, which is conducive to contemplation. Vipassana meditation, a simple and direct practice, helps the individ-

ual to examine the mind-body process through focused awareness. It
us to accept all aspects of living with equanimity and balance, which leads
to wisdom and compassion.

The austere setting seems to magnify the rugged beauty of the distant
mountains and the color of the sky at sunrise and sunset. The black,
star-filled night sky is awesome.

Dhamma Dena
HC-1, Box 250
Joshua Tree, CA 92252
(619) 362-4815

Accommodations: *Can host more than 50 men and women in various houses,
bunkhouses, trailers, and cabins; 4 outhouses (Japanese-style and nice); vegetarian
meals with community on pillows; morning stretching and meditation, and evening
meditation in nonretreat season; full meditation schedule during formal retreats; work
is part of the program here, people are asked to participate in large and small tasks;
open year-round; $20 a day.*

Directions: *Take Hwy. 62 North from Palm Springs to Joshua Tree. Approximately 3½ miles past the town, and 1 mile past the Highway Patrol, watch for
ANIMAL OASIS sign and airport, and turn left on Sunfair Rd. After 5 miles this road
veers a little to the left and becomes unpaved. Continue on it for 3–4 more miles.
Watch for VIPASSANA sign on left. Turn here and go to main building on left just
down the road.*

El Rancho del Obispo
(The Bishop's Ranch)
Healdsburg, CA

In 1947, the Episcopal Diocese of California bought 63 acres of the White family ranch and named it El Rancho del Obispo, the Bishop's Ranch, after Bishop Karl Morgan Block, who envisioned it initially as an Episcopal retreat. Over the years, it has enlarged its mission and serves all religious and nonprofit groups that seek a quiet, restful place for times of reflection.

Located in the lush wine country of Sonoma County, the buildings are on a knoll looking down to vineyards and across the wide valley where the Russian River flows. The expansive view across the green fields to the hills on the far side of the valley is the essence of tranquillity.

The ranch house is a brick Spanish-style mansion built by the Whites in the 1930s. An old-world courtyard adds charm to the two-story house, which has rooms for 33 guests. The large living room with beamed ceiling and a fieldstone fireplace can accommodate more than 50 people for meetings. The nearby Kip Cottage and five cabins give the ranch facilities a guest capacity of 90. There is a separate dining facility where a professional staff prepares excellent meals.

The adobe chapel at the edge of the lawns across from the ranch house was built in the 1950s. Inside, the arched altar is balanced by two narrow deep-blue windows—an intimate, quiet place for reflection and meditation. There are morning and evening prayer services, announced by a bell. Guests are welcome to join the few residents at the services. Choir groups come regularly from San Francisco, feeling a spiritual connection to the chapel and the beauty of the grounds.

A grass volleyball court and a large swimming pool are located near the cabins. The open fields and neat vineyards are inviting to walk in. Bird life is abundant.

El Rancho del Obispo
(The Bishop's Ranch)
5297 Westside Rd.
Healdsburg, CA 95448
(707) 433-2440

Accommodations: *Beds for 90 (33 in ranch house, 12 in Kip Cottage) and 5 cabins for men, women, and children (ranch house to be remodeled); buffet meals in modern refectory overlooking vineyards on this beautiful property; homemade breads, rolls, desserts; vegetables from own garden or local farmers; daily morning and evening prayer and Sunday Eucharist in lovely chapel; pool, volleyball, hiking on 63 acres and nearby roads and trails; many wineries nearby; open year-round; overnight without meals $25 per person, weeknight with meals $40, weekends 1 night and 3 meals, $50, 2 nights and 5 meals $70.*

Directions: *El Rancho del Obispo is 5 miles west of Hwy. 101 on Westside Rd. Coming north take Central Healdsburg exit and follow this until the first traffic light, then turn left under freeway. Follow Westside Rd. to sign on right. Coming south take Westside Rd.–Guerneville exit and proceed out Westside Rd.*

Esalen Institute
Big Sur, CA

The institute is one of the few places along Route 1 where adequate land on the ocean side provides natural protection for buildings from the sometimes raging and unforgiving waves. The Esalen grounds sit below the road like a private island; the western and southern edges of the property are steep rocky cliffs, 30 to 50 feet above the sea. The rocks offshore are home to seals, quail visit the gardens, and birds of seacoast and mountains feel equally at home. The landscape with its flowering bushes has the touch of a master gardener. Almost anything will grow in this mild climate.

If there is a center for the New Age that came upon U.S. society in the 1960s and was embraced gleefully by social revolutionaries who declared "Anything is better than what we have," Esalen must be it. It is considered one of the most important places providing fuel to the fires of change. In 1961, Michael Murphy used this oceanfront land owned by his family since 1910 to organize and build a meeting place where original thinkers could come to lead seminars on new ideas. Just as Murphy envisioned, there is an ongoing program of courses in education, religion, philosophy, and the physical and behavioral sciences that offers an interesting parallel to a Greek gymnasium. This center of emotional, mental, physical, and spiritual exploration is an experiment for the future and continues to invite well-known teachers and thinkers to share ideas.

The Esalen Indians who once lived here were attracted by the hot springs that come up from the rugged terrain. The sulfur water approaches 120 degrees and is piped into stone tubs built on the edge of a cliff wall. Here the views of sky and ocean on a clear night are like being at sea in the universe. Nudity is common in the baths, massage area, and swimming pool. A written notice reminds visitors that Esalen is a place of personal sanctuary with respect for the human body.

There are luxury rooms with private baths as well as sleeping bag space and community washrooms. Meals are served in the main dining room buffet-style. Snacks and hot drinks are generally available during the day. Just outside the dining room, there is a large deck with tables and chairs that encourages outside eating in good weather. From this deck, there is a view south to 20 miles of coastline.

Guests can attend courses or simply rent a room; enjoy the grounds, baths, and food; and structure their own private retreats.

Esalen Institute
Big Sur, CA 93920
(408) 667-3005 (Reservations)
(408) 667-3000 (General Information)

Accommodations: *Pleasant singles, doubles, and bunks for up to 100 men, women, and children with private or shared bath; sleeping bag spaces also available; early childhood program available ([408] 667-3026); tasty cafeteria-style vegetarian and nonvegetarian meals with much of the produce grown in Esalen's own organic garden, seating in dining room or on deck overlooking Pacific; workshops, seminars, work/study programs, invitational conferences in humanities and sciences that promote human values and potentials; extensive catalog available; swimming, hiking, unique hot springs available under open sky 24 hours a day (co-ed, swimsuits optional); bodywork of all kinds available by appointment; open year-round; room and board $95–$115 a day when available; scholarships available for courses; typical weekend, including program, $350; weeklong program $1,025; privacy zealously guarded by gatekeeper to prevent drop-ins.*

Directions: *45 miles south of Monterey on Rte. 1, and 11 miles south of the restaurant Nepenthe. A lighted sign on the ocean side marks the steep driveway: ESALEN INSTITUTE—BY RESERVATION ONLY.*

Franciscan Canticle
Sacred Heart Renewal Center
Victorville, CA

On the outskirts of Victorville, a complex of buildings that once served as a seminary for the Priests of the Sacred Heart was acquired in 1989 by the Franciscan Canticle. The center is located on 79 acres of the Mojave Desert and is surrounded by the distant San Bernadino Mountains. The mission of the Franciscans who live here is to provide an inspirational setting where artists can come to live, work, reflect, and experience mutual support.

The idea came from the collaborative thinking of a community of artists who envisioned a center for the development of spirituality and the arts. Father Edd Anthony, a member of the group, had been given a brochure about the property. He visited the area and determined it was not what he had in mind. The place was dry, sparsely inhabited, and unappealing. After the visit, he held a retreat for 80 nuns near Point Malibu. On a break, he walked to the ocean, still puzzled about the property, and prayed, "If You want me to go there, *You'll* have to tell me." The next day, an 88-year-old nun came up to him and said: "God has a message for you. . . . Go to the desert!"

Art can be used as a form of meditation that leads into a state of prayer. Breathing techniques and guided imagery help us to both relax and focus attention. The great Franciscan, St. Bonaventure, taught these processes in the Middle Ages. The centering effect of art helps us to see the world with appreciation, compassion, and love.

Regular retreats are held most weekends. The Franciscans act as hosts for those who have their own agenda. Local groups such as the Sierra Club,

Catholic Daughters of America, and the Knights of Columbus hold meetings in the conference rooms. Mass is celebrated in the chapel three times a week at 11:30 A.M. There is a Charismatic mass once a month. Private retreatants are welcome.

There are beds for 32 persons in double rooms with shared baths. The rooms are in two wings separated by a courtyard—the dining room at one end and the chapel and conference rooms at the other. A volleyball court, a tennis court, and a swimming pool are located behind the buildings. The desert is just beyond with plenty of space to roam.

An artist-in-residence program is planned for 1993. Each artist will have a private room, a studio, and a shared bath.

Franciscan Canticle, Inc.
13333 Palmdale Rd.
Victorville, CA 92392
(619) 241-2538

Accommodations: 32 beds in 16 rooms and 6 artist-in-residence studios for men and women; family-style dinners across courtyard in main dining room, pick-up breakfasts and lunches; chapel open for daily prayer and meditation; just in planning stages during our visit for a $1,000-a-month Christian Artist-in-Residence Program with private room and studio; pool, tennis, basketball, volleyball; open year-round; $65 a weekend.

Directions: Take Palmdale exit from Rte. 15. Follow Palmdale Rd. west about 3½ miles and watch for sign on left. Very commercial road; sign is hard to spot. If you reach Hostess Thrift Bakery you've just passed the entrance.

Green Gulch Farm Zen Center
Muir Beach, CA

In the early 1970s, the San Francisco Zen Center was looking for a country location where its members could live, work, and practice meditation. During the same period, the Nature Conservancy was looking for a group to maintain a farm, part of 535 upland acres deeded to it by George Wheelright III, whose intent was to preserve the property in its unspoiled and natural condition and maintain the plant and animal life.

This superb land is only 25 minutes by car from San Francisco and is located between Mill Valley and Muir Beach. Made up of low hills and ridges, the property has half a mile of ocean frontage. Surrounded by the Golden Gate National Recreation Area, Green Gulch is an exquisite example of California's coastland, accessible by the two-lane winding Route 1, where slow, cautious driving is not only intelligent but a necessity. An arrangement was made for the Zen Center to buy 115 acres on the condition that it would be farmed in perpetuity and remain open to the public.

As part of its practice, the Zen community demonstrates that Buddhist attention to detail in land stewardship produces good crops, a spiritual reward in itself. Green Gulch Farm has become a showcase, growing superb-quality produce, herbs, and flowers that are prized in the Bay Area. The 15 acres of carefully tended fields with rainbow rows of lettuce—more than a dozen kinds—are a source of fresh supply to area restaurants, including the affiliated and famous Greens Restaurant in San Francisco.

The resident community of 50 adults and 8 children, while keeping the farm going, also have an active schedule of retreat programs, classes, and gardening workshops. There are two daily zazen periods, one in the morning and the other in late afternoon. Part of a former barn is used as the sitting room; the rustic wooden building with polished wooden floors, dimly lighted by small windows, is quiet and appropriate. Statues of the Buddha are graced by flowers, candles, and artifacts.

The handcrafted Oriental-style Lindisfarne Guesthouse, which also serves as a conference center, has nails only under the plaster walls in the Sheetrock. All the wood was hand-planed, some of it oak from a tree that fell at Tassajara (the mountain retreat center), some Port Orford cedar, often used in Japanese buildings. The two-story structure's rooms flow together toward the 30-foot atrium in the center where guests can sit around the woodstove on chairs and sofas. The rooms are elegant and comfortable. Each room shares a modern bathroom.

Green Gulch Farm Zen Center
1601 Shoreline Hwy.
Muir Beach, CA 94965
(415) 383-3134

Accommodations: *The beautiful handcrafted guesthouse has 12 rooms surrounding a 30-foot atrium, and 3 rooms elsewhere, all doubles, for men and women, and a suite elsewhere on the property that can accommodate 1 family; delicious vegetarian meals with much produce from the farm's extensive gardens; daily meditation and service with community, with a special Sunday program including lecture; meditation instruction available; meditation retreats, Buddhist study classes, workshops, gardening classes, conference facilities; 15-minute walk to beach through gardens and fields; sauna, pool, library, unique teahouse, hiking trails; open year-round; $40– $90 a day plus about $5 for each meal; guest student program $15 a day. Reservations required for overnight stay.*

Directions: *Hwy. 101 to Stinson Beach, Rte. 1 turnoff. Follow Rte. 1 (Shoreline Hwy.) 2½ miles to turnoff for Muir Woods. At this point follow the dotted center line to left (State Rte. 1) for 2 more miles to Green Gulch Farm on left.*

Harbin Hot Springs
Middletown, CA

The New Age is alive and well, growing and thriving on this 1,160-acre retreat in a remote mountain setting. The center is built around natural mineral hot springs known for soothing and healing properties, where the water is captured in large pools open for bathing 24 hours a day. The community accepts the responsibility of preserving the springs as a sanctuary where others may come for rest, reflection, and renewal.

The property was originally purchased by a community member in 1972 and has become part of the Heart Consciousness Church, which espouses the holistic health movement, natural healing, the human potential movement, and universal spirituality. "We're all in this together," one person observed, "so let's work things out peacefully."

About 130 people live here sharing the housekeeping, landscaping, and maintenance. The community is open to individuals and families who might be interested in becoming resident members.

There are four buildings available for groups of 14 to 300 people who attend the various workshops and education programs offered. The school of massage and shiatsu, which blends the Eastern and Western traditions, offers state-approved certification.

There are more than 50 single and double rooms for guests. Accommodations range from rooms with full or half-bath to dormitories with mattresses only. Bring your own linens or a sleeping bag. Kitchen space is available for cooking. There is also a restaurant offering three meals a day and a general store with basic items. Camping is permitted in designated areas.

There are many hiking paths and trails through the property, some quite demanding. The air at 1,700 feet is pure and invigorating. "This is a good place for healing," one member said. "We are caretakers of a sanctuary. . . . We need to be quiet, focused, and centered. We are taking care of Mother Earth; then we can take care of each other."

Harbin Hot Springs
P.O. Box 782
Middletown, CA 95461
(707) 987-2477

Accommodations: *Dorms, singles, doubles, and camping for men, women, and children in this unique New Age community; vegetarian meals that are hearty and delicious available in their restaurant, or cook your own vegetarian meals in community kitchen; Vipassana meditation daily, courses, conferences, Saturday-night purification fire, sacred singing on Sunday at 7:30 P.M.; full moon meditation; hike, camp, explore, sunbathe (clothing optional) on 1,160 acres of secluded forest, meadows, streams bordered by Mount Harbin and state forest land; 2 large natural warm mineral pools, hot mineral pool, sauna, 2 stream-fed cold plunges, and a large cold swimming pool (co-ed dressing room) open 24 hours a day; massage therapists, shiatsu center; open year-round; camping $10–$15 a day, dorm $18 a day; double with private bath $115, but they supply just one towel, others must be rented; meals separate; bring flashlight.*

Directions: *Rte. 29 North from Calistoga to Middletown. Left at the stoplight and right at Barnes St. Follow 4 miles and stay on left at fork.*

Immaculate Heart Community
Center for Spiritual Renewal
Santa Barbara, CA

The center is located in a large stone manor house and shares 26 acres of beautiful grounds with La Casa de Maria (see page 46) in the Montecito neighborhood just below San Ysidro Ranch. A small group of Immaculate Heart Community women live here; the headquarters of the 189-member community is in Los Angeles.

In response to the call for renewal from Vatican II in the late 1960s, the Immaculate Heart Community tried to adapt to a new form of religious life integrating the richness of past history with contemporary circumstances and understanding. The modifications from past traditions included a choice of work, a modified dress code, and active involvement in social justice. The Cardinal of Los Angeles reacted by issuing a decree to the community requiring uniform dress and daily prayer, work limited to education, and cooperation with the Church, which at this time was closing schools in poor neighborhoods, many of them schools where the sisters were teaching. The sisters were shocked and hurt by the authoritarian mandate. In 1969, a majority of the sisters declared independence, announcing they would become "a noncanonical community of religious persons." The gentle strength of the community is evident as its members look forward to an ever-changing future. As one said, "It is true to say the Immaculate Heart Community is something it always was, and it is also becoming something it never was."

The center has rooms with private baths for six guests on retreat. The resident community makes every effort to provide warm hospitality in an atmosphere of gentle silence. Community members are available for conversation but otherwise visitors structure their own time. A nondenominational evening prayer meeting is scheduled after dinner and guests are welcome. There is a large selection of tapes and books available. Breakfast and lunch may be picked up from the well-stocked kitchen; the evening meal is served family-style with everyone sitting down together at the large dining table.

The manor house has an elegant wood interior and is comfortably furnished and carefully maintained. The serene atmosphere is easy to adjust to and difficult to leave. As one guest wrote: "This is the only place where I can give in to myself—one of the most valuable gifts of my life." Another wrote: "Home away from home, like Grandmother's, where everything is homemade."

Immaculate Heart Community
Center for Spiritual Renewal
888 San Ysidro Ln.
Santa Barbara, CA 93108
(805) 969-2474

Accommodations: 6 lovely, spacious bedrooms with private baths for men and women in this gracious mansion, and a 3-bedroom hermitage; delicious pick-up breakfast and lunch—with oranges and juice, from the center's own trees, and homemade chocolate chip cookies, for example—and dinner with the community each evening, followed by an ecumenical night prayer together; 26 acres of beautiful grounds for walking, and a county trail, a 3–4 hour walk, adjoining property; nice books everywhere, including a comfortable library; Corita Kent drawings on walls; open year-round Wednesday to Sunday; suggested donation: $45 a person, $55 for married couples.

Directions: Rte. 101 to San Ysidro exit. Follow San Ysidro Rd. to E. Valley Rd. (second light). Turn right on E. Valley for ²/₁₀ mile to El Bosque Rd. Turn left on San Ysidro La. and go 1 mile to the center.

Incarnation Priory
Berkeley, CA

In a northern Berkeley neighborhood, near Peet's Coffee Shop and the Thunderbird Bookstore, an experiment in monasticism has flourished since 1979. It was then, following the Rule of St. Benedict, that Episcopalian and Roman Catholic monks joined together to pray, work, study, and live. Though retaining their separate liturgies and identities, they co-own and co-manage this three-story building. Each of the groups maintains its own rhythm, customs, and constitutions. There are currently five monks of the Episcopalian Order of the Holy Cross and three Roman Catholic Camaldolese. The monks support themselves in various ways: one teaches, another is a practicing engineer, one is a counselor, some do editing and writing, others do parish work such as preaching, retreats, adult education, and spiritual direction.

They have an active guest ministry, and keep three rooms available for visitors. Kitchen facilities provide pick-up breakfast and lunch. Guests may join the community for dinner at 7 P.M., preceded by a social period in the common room. These meals are excellent and an opportune time to meet and chat with these dedicated men.

Berkeley is built on gently sloping terrain that joins the Pacific at San Francisco Bay, and is one of the great intellectual centers of the United States. It is the site of what is referred to as the brightest light in the University of California's education system, a school that regularly vies with Harvard for the title of the most balanced and distinguished university in this country.

In this atmosphere of high cultural achievement where new ideas and attitudes are encouraged and enlarged, it seems auspicious that monks representing two different churches are living together in active peace. The catchphrase of the community—"Unity through diversity"—helps them to follow the message of Christ: "Not for those alone do I pray but also for those who through their words put their faith in me. May they all be one as you Father are in me and I in you, so may they be one in us. . . ."

Incarnation Priory
1601 Oxford St.
Berkeley, CA 94709
(415) 548-3406

Accommodations: *For men, women, and children, there are 3 rooms, 1 with twin beds, and a separate apartment with 2 doubles in this 10-unit apartment house in downtown Berkeley that has been made into a monastery; dinner with community following vespers if you like, and pick-up breakfast and lunch; regular prayer services and Eucharist; a good place for people coming for study, conferences, etc., in Berkeley; open year-round; $30 a day for one person, $45 a couple; $5 for dinner.*

Directions: *Rte. 101 to Bay Bridge. Stay left and watch for Berkeley signs. Take University Ave. exit and follow University to Shattuck and turn left. Follow Shattuck to Cedar and turn right on Cedar for 2 blocks to Oxford. Right on Oxford and left into first driveway (Episcopal church parking lot).*

Isis Oasis
Geyserville, CA

Named after the Egyptian goddess of nature and fertility and located on ten acres, Isis Oasis attempts to bridge the gap between ancient cultures and the New Age. With an affinity to the International Fellowship of Isis, this retreat promotes goddess-consciousness and the feminine principle as a way to restore balance and harmony to Mother Earth.

Once a Native American ceremonial ground, then a Baha'i school, the property was acquired in 1981 by Lora Vigne and partner Paul Ramses, who began to restore and refurbish the buildings. They have added an Egyptian temple designed with the acoustics of an instrument to focus the energy of the place. The eclectic nature of the plan unfolding here is amazing. Visitors can choose between the comfortable, semi-Victorian main house, with a full kitchen and private rooms, a separate self-contained cottage for families or couples, a room in a wine barrel with the faint aroma of Zinfandel, a tepee, or a yurt. These accommodations are not far from the redwood meeting-dining room, which has rest rooms and a fireplace. A large conference room is available for groups up to 100. There is a swimming pool and also hot tubs on various decks of some of the residential buildings.

Behind the quaint farmhouse (the private residence of the proprietors) is an aviary of peacocks, doves, and Himalayan pheasants. More cages contain ocelots (bred for years by Lora) as well as bobcats in a separate enclosure, and there is a corral containing an emu and a llama named Dali. These elegant animals illustrate the great variety in the world and show that it is possible to live in harmony.

The Oasis is an integral part of the small farming town of Geyserville, which works hard at developing community spirit. The local Chamber of Commerce holds a dinner each month and hundreds of people attend.

Private retreatants and guests attending the seminars can wander through an orchard to the Russian River nearby or enjoy the ambience of small-town life while sampling the diversity of Egyptian culture. "The goddess movement is coming in," Lora points out. "The feminine concept of softer energy to save the planet, to be more considerate of others, is beginning to emerge." Given man's history in the 20th century and the aggressive actions of the United States at the beginning of the 1990s, there would seem to be a good deal of room for a more feminine approach.

Isis Oasis
20889 Geyserville Ave.
Geyserville, CA 95441
(707) 857-3524

Accommodations: *Beds for a maximum of 80 men and women in a variety of accommodations from yurts, tepees, retreat house, lodge, cottage, tower house, vineyard house, trailer, to dorm and loft space; breakfast included and lunch and dinner can be arranged; 12 × 12 × 12 ft. Egyptian temple can be used for ceremonies (many weddings have been performed here), and a 30 × 60 ft. theater for 100 people is available for workshops and meetings; owner collects exotic birds and animals, including a llama, an emu, black swans, pigmy goats, bobcats, ocelots, serval cats; workshops on Egyptian arts and rituals; 10 acres; swimming pool; lovely Egyptian gift and book shop; closed first 3 weeks December; prices range from $40 a day for a couple for the tepee to $100 a day for a couple in the cottage.*

Directions: *Isis Oasis is 80 miles north of San Francisco on Hwy. 101; look for* TO ROUTE 128 EAST, GEYSERVILLE *exit sign. Follow Frontage Rd. into Geyserville. See sign at first driveway on left.*

Krotona Institute of Theosophy
Ojai, CA

The beautiful Ojai Valley of Southern California, which was used as a backdrop for the fabled Shangri-La during the filming of James Hilton's novel *Lost Horizon*, is the 118-acre setting of the Krotona Institute, a school composed of members of the Theosophical Society. This worldwide organization came here in 1924 to establish a center for the study of Theosophy (the wisdom of God), which is a body of ideas from religions and philosophies from India, China, Greece, and the Middle East, and from scientific discoveries, past and present. Convinced that belief should be a result of individual study, experience, and insight rather than acceptance of traditional dogma, the society sees every religion as an expression of divine wisdom, to be studied rather than dismissed or condemned, and to be practiced rather than preached. Theosophy is nonsectarian, nonpolitical, and nondogmatic. It espouses three objectives: to form a nucleus of all persons without regard to race, creed, sex, caste, or color; to encourage the study of all religions, philosophy, and science; and to investigate the laws of nature and the latent power we all possess.

The Spanish-style buildings with red-tile roofs include a lecture hall, library, music room, and offices. Staff members live in nearby houses. There is a guesthouse for society members who come for business meetings and programs put on by an international faculty well versed in Theosophy.

A regular event program for members of the society includes weekend retreats that provide for periods of meditative silence. A resident student program offers eight weeks of training and study and a work/study program for longer periods. A series of courses is offered, one day a week for a period of weeks or months, dealing with varying topics such as "Discovering the Feminine Values in Our Lives" and "The Occult World."

On a hilltop looking toward Ojai Valley and the surrounding mountains, with the tall graceful trees and white stucco buildings surrounded by well-tended hedges and bushes, the Krotona Institute is a serene setting for philosophical and spiritual reflection.

Krotona Institute of Theosophy
2 Krotona Hill
Ojai, CA 93023
(805) 646-2653

Accommodations: *Guesthouse for members only. For membership information contact: The Theosophical Society in America, 1926 North Main Street, Wheaton, IL 60189-0270, (708) 668-1571; open Monday–Friday 9 A.M.–noon and 1–4 P.M. for day visitors to grounds and library; bookstore open 10 A.M.–4 P.M. Monday– Saturday and 1–4 P.M. on Sunday. Special programs also offered.*

Directions: *Rte. 101 to Ojai exit, Rte. 33; go 12–13 miles through towns of Casitas and Oakview; take the first left after sign for Ojai city limits (watch for Villanova School on right just before turn), and then take the next left onto Krotona Hill and follow sign to library and bookstore.*

La Casa de Maria
Santa Barbara, CA

The entrance of this 26-acre retreat winds through the wooded neighborhood of Montecito, past orange and lemon trees and one of the largest eucalyptus trees in the county. The abundance of outstanding and unusual trees and bushes on the grounds includes a monkey puzzle tree and a star pine. Along a gently curving road, the buildings resemble haciendas with white walls and tiled roofs. A strumming guitar at siesta time would complete the picture.

This tranquil setting is where an energetic director and staff organize and run a full program of spiritually oriented single-day and weekend retreats. The topics range from AA to prayer and dance workshops and a "work weekend" when guests help to maintain the facilities by painting, gardening, and cooking while laughing and praying together. This is a popular gathering place for administrators and union officials to come together in a neutral environment and find solutions. There are rooms for more than 150 people in motel-like wings and most have private baths. The dining room with adjoining terrace serves meals buffet-style. By all accounts the food gets high marks.

The Casa's history goes back to 1780, when the king of Spain granted the land to the Franciscan missions and the padres built a way station for traveling missionaries. The land came under private ownership in the 1800s, when citrus groves were planted. La Casa was a grand estate for the Wack family, who raised horses here in the early 1900s. The Sisters of the Immaculate Heart purchased the property and took possession on Easter Monday 1943. A large donation in 1955 made it possible to build a 24-room unit where married couples could come for retreats, the first in the United

States for that specific purpose. The chapel was also built at that time, and has a window looking out on a huge gnarled oak with a life-size crucifixion in front of it.

During the 1970s, the Center for Spiritual Renewal, which shares the grounds here, was founded. It is managed by an independent board of trustees whose mandate from the sisters is to keep the Casa in perpetuity as a retreat center. Every year a donation is received from a Swiss visitor who on his initial retreat here was asked neither if he could afford to pay nor his religious affiliation. The money is used for scholarships for those who cannot afford to pay.

This is a place of healing and conciliation. One of the staff commented, "We urge those in conflict always to listen to the other side; don't allow rigid idealism to become brutalization, like the Crusades and the conflict in the Middle East."

La Casa de Maria
800 El Bosque Rd.
Santa Barbara, CA 93108
(805) 969-5031

Accommodations: *For men and women, 42 spacious rooms with 3 beds and private bath; 2 dorms, one with 12 beds and the other with 40 beds and private kitchen; tasty buffet meals; all faiths welcome to use chapel; walks, tennis, pool on 26 acres of lush beautiful grounds, meditation chapel; open year-round; room $35 a day, board for private retreats suggested donation: $20 a day; schedule of fees for groups available.*

Directions: *Rte. 101 to San Ysidro Rd. exit. Follow San Ysidro to E. Valley Rd. (second light). Turn right on E. Valley for ²⁄₁₀ mile to El Bosque Rd., and left on El Bosque to La Casa.*

Manresa Jesuit Retreat Center
Azusa, CA

Just a few miles from one of Southern California's ten-lane expressways, in the town of Azusa, where houses and condominium developments continue for miles, the road into Manresa is bordered by 90-foot royal palms. The secluded 10-acre retreat, with an elaborate Norman-style château built in 1932, was bought by the Jesuits in 1947. Their initial mission was to provide an opportunity for prayer and spiritual growth, and this continues today as they offer a full schedule of retreats for nearby parishes and others who are interested. There is an annual silent retreat, which some men have been coming to for 25 years. Extensive coverage is provided for AA and Al-Anon groups. The eight Jesuits who live here organize and staff the programs. The property and buildings are exceptionally well maintained.

Over the years, 70 double rooms have been built that have beds for 140 guests. These additions, called hermitages, are separate from the château, but are only steps away along landscaped walks. The dining room, where three meals a day are prepared by a professional staff, is in the main house. There is a large, comfortable wood-paneled reading room and library started in 1960. The book selections reflect the breadth of the late Father John Shepherd, on staff since 1959, and range from poetry to architecture to religion—and should satisfy the most discriminating reader. This is a very restful room. There is a swimming pool, and outdoor stations of the cross wind through pine trees and flowering bushes. The landscaping is quite elegant.

The nursery that surrounds the retreat covers 600 acres. It is a pleasure to wander along the pathways and admire the arrangements of bushes, plants, and flowers that grow so readily in this mild climate.

The center was named after the town in northeastern Spain where St. Ignatius of Loyola spent 11 months (1522–23) in solitude and prayer developing the famous spiritual exercises that eventually led to the founding of the Society of Jesus.

During a discussion of retreat themes, a priest said: "We point out that peace is a consequence of right order; we should be working toward justice and fairness in our lives, remembering that for every virtue there are two vices, the two extremes." He went on to tell of a man who said he was an extremist: "I'm in the extreme center!" "That's fine," the priest agreed, "as long as it's not *dead* center."

Manresa Jesuit Retreat House
801 E. Foothill Blvd.
P.O. Box K
Azusa, CA 91702-1330
(818) 969-1848

Accommodations: *Singles and doubles with private baths for men and women in a variety of small older rooms overlooking the lovely landscaped gardens or new accommodations on a lower part of the property; 3 hearty meals at round tables in pleasant dining room in main mansion; mass daily plus prayer services for the frequent retreat programs; 10 acres of gardens and garden walks, surrounded by 600-acre nursery for walking; swimming pool; beautiful library; open year-round; $50 a day.*

Directions: *About 12 miles east of Pasadena on Rte. 210. Take Citrus Ave. exit. Follow Citrus north (left) 1 mile to Foothill; left on Foothill and watch on right for* MANRESA RETREAT *sign and* MONROVIA NURSERY *sign (if they've not relocated).*

Mercy Center
Burlingame, CA

The Mercy Center is located a few blocks from downtown Burlingame, a suburb south of San Francisco. It is approached through a neighborhood of neat, trim houses and a long winding driveway into the 40-acre enclosure. The imposing main building, the Mother House of the Sisters of Mercy, was built in 1929. The elegant look of the building masks its size. Major additions were made in 1962 to house novitiates, and in the early 1980s the mission of the order was redefined to make it available for conferences and retreat work.

The condition of the building inside is a reflection of the manicured grounds outside. There are 92 rooms, many with private baths, for 100 people. Two dining rooms serve excellent food cafeteria-style. There is elevator access to the sleeping floors above and the conference rooms on a lower level. Mass is said in the large chapel, just off the main entrance, five days out of seven. There is a meditation room, near the conference rooms, reminiscent of a Buddhist temple, an ecumenical acknowledgment of the chaplain, Father Thomas Hand, who spent 28 years in Japan before he joined the center in 1984. Father Hand's hobby is designing meditation paths. His first creation took him six years to carve out of a hillside in Japan. He has constructed three meditation walks on the center's grounds: Waterway, Woodway, and Wonderway. These are a delight to follow—pathways bridging the spirituality of East and West.

There are regularly scheduled 12-step programs, as well as weekend and weeklong retreats that study the Enneagram, explore intensive meditation, and offer periods of private time for prayer and renewal. There is a 30-week program of spiritual direction modeled on that of St. Ignatius; individuals meet weekly with their group to discuss integrating spirituality into every-day life.

Since the early 1980s, the Taizé religious community has been coming annually to Taizé West, as the Mercy Center is also known, for a week to sing and pray. This ecumenical community from France, known for its singing and helping in a search for life's meaning, includes Catholics and Protestants from 20 countries. This popular event is so appealing to young people that sleeping bag space has to be assigned; guests use the community washrooms and take meals in the dining rooms. The Taizé phenomenon is encouraged and followed up with monthly concerts of this unique music and draws hundreds regularly.

Mercy Center
2300 Adeline Dr.
Burlingame, CA 94010
(415) 340-7474

Accommodations: *92 private rooms for men and women, and 13 meeting rooms; cafeteria-style meals; mass 5 days; meditation in chapel Monday–Friday; very popular Taizé singing in evening first Friday of each month; 3 Japanese paths for walking created by Jesuit Tom Hand, who also created the Eastern Meditation Room in the center; 500-year-old California oaks on 40 acres; tennis courts, pool, bookstore, art exhibits; open year-round; $36 a day for private retreat; $44 for groups who also use meeting rooms.*

Directions: *Mercy Center is 4 miles south of the San Francisco airport. Take Hwy. 101 to Broadway exit. Follow Broadway to El Camino. Right on El Camino to third light at Adeline. Left on Adeline a few blocks to Mercy Center on right.*

Mission San Luis Rey Retreat
San Luis Rey, CA

Founded in 1798 by Spanish Franciscan fathers, by 1830 the "King of the Missions" had become the largest and most populous of all the California missions. By working with the local Native American tribes, the padres managed to cultivate oranges, olives, and grapes on a large scale in addition to raising 27,000 cattle and 26,000 sheep. The mission became the home for more than 2,000 Native Americans. In 1834 Mexico passed laws that caused a period of disruption, and by 1846 the padres abandoned the mission and the property wound up in the hands of relatives of the Mexican governor. California became a state in 1850. Then in 1865 President Abraham Lincoln declared that the sale of mission lands was illegal and he restored to the Catholic church 65 acres of the present property. By the late 1800s, the Franciscans had returned and begun the work of restoration.

Over the past 100 years, the buildings have been restored, the grounds reclaimed, and a museum of artifacts established. Reminders of past grandeur are everywhere. The brick walkways pass by the oldest giant pepper tree in California, planted in 1830, and meander through Spanish-style courtyards with graceful arches. The mission walls are accentuated with flowering bushes.

This is a peaceful place where visitors can escape the bustle of Southern California outside the white walls. There are double-occupancy rooms for 108 persons with communal washrooms. Excellent food is served in the large, charming dining room with decorated beamed ceilings.

The Franciscan community that lives here offers a full schedule of retreats. The topics deal with addiction recovery, charismatic healing, divorce and separation, engaged encounters, and marriage. Weekend retreats for women and a week for religious sisters are also offered. Private retreatants can be accommodated if there is space available.

There is daily mass at 7 A.M. in the mission church, where the original decorations have been restored. The mission exists as an important reminder of California's historic past, which now serves present-day needs as a spiritual haven.

Mission San Luis Rey Retreat
P.O. Box 409
San Luis Rey, CA 92068
(619) 757-3659

Accommodations: 108 beds in very worn doubles for men, women, and children (only in groups); 3 meals available for $6 each in old seminary dining room with hand-painted ceiling beams; mass available frequently in community chapel or in lovely old mission chapel; the old mission that is part of this complex is open for visitors to tour and is beautifully preserved—it is a unique experience to be able to stay on these grounds; swimming pool, basketball, volleyball, picnic tables, walking, orange, lemon, and avocado trees; guided retreats for the religious; open year-round; $22.50 a day, double occupancy for rooms.

Directions: I-5 to Mission Ave. exit in Oceanside; follow Mission Ave. (Hwy. 76) east 3½ miles to Rancho del Oro Dr. (watch for white mission buildings and blue dome on left).

Monastery of Mount Tabor
Redwood Valley, CA

This Eastern rite contemplative community of a dozen monks has lived on these 200 sloping, hilltop acres in the coastal range of Northern California since the mid-1970s. Mount Tabor, named after the mountain where tradition says Christ was transfigured, is a Byzantine monastery of the Ukrainian Catholic church. Their exceptional liturgy with all its fervor, beauty, and grace is the focal point of each day. The three services last about five hours in all. The experience is very powerful: beautifully sung prayers, some prostrations, clouds of incense, candles being lighted and extinguished, bearded monks moving about the altar dressed in magnificent vestments, rich full voices filling the small church. There are no distractions; everything, including the elegant icons on the walls, focuses one's attention on the reason for being here: profound divine worship.

There are rooms for 16 guests in a guesthouse up the hill from the church. The simple, spare rooms have a single bed, desk, chair, and sink and share baths. There is a kitchen for making hot drinks or snacks, which guests should bring. Regular meals are taken with the monks in the dining room just below the church, and in cool weather there is a roaring fire in the fireplace. The windows look out on the gardens below and the hills beyond. During the noon meal one of the monks reads aloud from a spiritual text. The food is hearty and nutritious. Once a week fasting is observed and only bread is available. Every Friday the monks pick up leftovers from local food stores, and some neighbors send food regularly.

Guests are expected to attend all services and meals and to help with some of the work. A monk can be available for spiritual guidance but this should be prearranged. Hiking on the mountain property is rigorous. The views down the valley are exceptionally peaceful from this mountain of spirituality.

Monastery of Mount Tabor
P.O. Box 217
17001 Tomki Rd.
Redwood Valley, CA 95470
(707) 485-8959

Accommodations: *Guesthouse for men and women with 10 singles, plus 2 dorms; 3 buffet meals in refectory with fireplace and view of hills (1 meal a day during Lent); stunning chapel with frequent, extensive, beautiful services and voices with prostrations at each service; 200 acres of mountains and valleys; guests are required to attend all services and meals, help monks in their work, and share in their silence; open year-round except 1 week each month; minimum suggested donation: $20 a day.*

Directions: *Hwy. 101 North approximately 6 miles north of Ukiah, to West Rd. exit. Turn right (east) on West Rd. about 3 miles to end, then left on Tomki 4–5 miles to monastery on right. You're close when you get up into the hills.*

Mount Baldy Zen Center
Mount Baldy, CA

Surrounded by the Angeles National Forest at an altitude of 6,500 feet in the San Gabriel Mountains, the Mount Baldy Zen Center was founded in 1971 by Kyozan Joshua Sasaki Roshi only 35 miles from Los Angeles. The road to the center climbs upward in a torturous series of switchbacks that, on a clear day, afford spectacular panoramas through the mountain passes. The buildings, on a 4½-acre site once used as a Boy Scout camp, have been repaired and reclaimed. They hug the mountainside, unpretentious but efficient; stone-marked paths connect the buildings among the pine and fir trees.

A community of seven lives here and maintains the property for the scheduled Rinzai Zen training periods. The *seichu*, an intensive three-month practice period, is offered in both winter and summer. The rigorous daily schedule begins at 3 A.M. and lasts till 9 P.M. It includes two meditation periods, to begin and end the day, work practice for about eight hours, and three vegetarian meals. Regularly scheduled weeklong intensive retreats (*sesshins*) are held simultaneously during *seichu*. During the spring and fall, the schedule is less formal, but zazen periods are held morning and evening. Weekend programs are offered for beginners. Visitors should bring a sleeping bag, towels, hiking boots, and work clothes. This is an open center, cloistered only during retreats.

An introduction to Zen practice with meditation, instruction, discussion, and vegetarian lunch is scheduled on most Saturdays from 9 A.M. to 12:30 P.M.

Most visitors live dormitory-style using a communal bathhouse. The simplicity of the accommodations reflects the emphasis on Zen practice and is designed to reduce self-centeredness, do away with personal wants and feelings, and help visitors enter into the community; simple living facilitates clearing the mind.

"Following these Buddhist disciplines," one monk said, "leads to a wisdom that penetrates the nature and reasons for the universe and ourselves, the how and why the world exists, a state of awareness like awakening from sleep, and there is an awakening beyond that."

Mount Baldy Zen Center
P.O. Box 429
Mount Baldy, CA 91759
(714) 985-6410

Accommodations: *For men and women, a guest cabin for private retreat or quiet weekend, 4 cabins with 8 beds each, and several more cabins for a total of 45 beds; a washroom at each end of camp; outhouses; vegetarian meals, in silence during retreat periods; different methods of meditation practice are offered each season; daily chanting, meditation, and work periods; most Saturday mornings there is Visitors Day, with instruction and lunch; Jacuzzi, hot tub for 10; this is Forest Service property with lots of hiking trails in the mountains at 6,500 feet; open for guests year-round, except during weeklong intensive retreats; less formal in spring and fall; $15–$20 a day as part of community; guest cabin $35 a day.*

Directions: *Mount Baldy Zen Center is 1 hour east of Los Angeles and 35 minutes from the Indian Hill exit off Rte. 10 (15–17 miles). Left on Indian Hill, right on Foothill; left on Mills, which flows into Mt. Baldy Rd., which twists and turns high up into mountains.*

Mount Calvary Monastery and Retreat House

Santa Barbara, CA

On a rocky ledge in the foothills of the Santa Ynez Mountains, 1,250 feet above Santa Barbara, Mount Calvary offers breathtaking views of the Pacific Coast. On a clear day you can see north 40 miles to Point Magoo and south 25 miles to the Channel Islands. The natural cliffs on one side go down to Rattlesnake Canyon, on the other to the switchback road that winds up through an affluent neighborhood.

The monks are of the Order of the Holy Cross, an Episcopalian monastic community in the Benedictine tradition founded in New York City in 1884. They acquired this property in 1947 after searching up and down the coast. It was little more than a building shell when Father Karl Tiedemann found it, but he succeeded in raising the money to buy it. Known for his fund-raising ability, he wanted as his epitaph "And the beggar died." Father Tiedemann rests peacefully; a fellow monk noted he even got a free funeral.

The monastery is superbly constructed, with white stucco walls and a red-tile roof. The main entrance, through a large foyer with polished wood floors, has Spanish colonial antique furnishings under beamed ceilings. The room and central corridor are decorated with outstanding religious art and artifacts, including a carved wooden altar trimmed in gold leaf.

The monks sing the canonical hours in a separate chapel room and guests are welcome. A charming inner courtyard is dominated by a large sculpted iron cross. Fruit trees and flowering bushes grow in this protected area and some of the guest rooms open out onto it. Picture windows have glorious views of the Pacific. At night, the lights of Santa Barbara reach to the ocean's edge.

The monastery was founded as a retreat house and as a seat of spirituality from which the monks could go out to preach. They regularly descend from their mountain to Trinity Church in downtown Santa Barbara to prepare and serve meals for the homeless. There are 11 double rooms and 8 singles for retreatants. From time to time a "working retreat" is offered when individuals and groups donate time and skill to improving the facility. People of every religious denomination are welcome.

The Great Silence is observed from Compline, the last prayer service of the day, until breakfast. This quiet period enhances the experience of the location, an ocean of limitless space.

Mount Calvary Monastery and Retreat House
P.O. Box 1296
Santa Barbara, CA 93102
(805) 962-9855

Accommodations: 30 men, women, and children can be accommodated in 11 doubles and 8 singles in this stunning mansion high in the hills overlooking the Pacific; tasty buffet meals in refectory; Eucharist and prayer 4 times daily; working retreat to donate time and skills to retreat house is offered; monthly meal for homeless at Trinity Church in town; mountain hiking in Rattlesnake Canyon, a nature preserve that extends for 20 miles; library; bookstore 9–5 Monday–Saturday; closed last 2 weeks in August; suggested donation: $50 a day; visits normally limited to a week.

Directions: San Ysidro exit from Rte. 101 to 192 West (E. Valley Rd.). Left at second stoplight and follow 192 West for 4–5 miles over winding residential roads to El Cielito Rd. Turn right onto El Cielito (and at first stop sign watch carefully so you stay on El Cielito) to Gibraltar Rd. and right on Gibraltar 7/10 mile up mountain to chain link fence on left and drive to monastery. New signs being installed to help you find your way.

nt Madonna Center

Watsonville, CA

On a sloping hilltop with a sweeping, panoramic view of Monterey Bay, the Mount Madonna Center sits on 355 acres of meadows and forests. Situated equidistant between Watsonville and Gilroy, this is an international community of 60 adults and 40 children. Followers of the yogi Baba Hari Dass acquired the former cattle ranch in the 1970s and established a spiritual community with education as its primary focus and spiritual growth and character development as underlying themes. The core component is the study and practice of yoga, which they believe is not a religion but a spiritual path. "Yoga's basic disciplines are essentially the same as Catholicism, Buddhism, or any other great spiritual path," a spokesperson said. "Each has its own shadings or variations. We here are concerned with what is basic, true, and timeless; we're not concerned with separating ourselves from others or saying we are different than others."

The center's 30 buildings were financed as they were built. The redwood community building, facing the majestic western view, is the heart of the complex, with the kitchen and dining room, classrooms for the 100-plus students from kindergarten through high school, and administrative offices. Nearby is the seminar building, which is big enough for groups of 300 on weekend programs. The well-stocked and inviting library is in a separate building. Along the winding roadways are staff housing and guest facilities interspersed with gardens.

People here are friendly, cheerful, and happy to meet visitors. The excellent vegetarian food is served cafeteria-style and is carefully prepared with nutrition in mind. There is a variety of guest accommodations in many of the buildings as well as a cottage and guesthouse, or you may use your own tent or van. The property has acres of open meadows and redwood forests for hiking. The center also features a lake and volleyball and basketball courts.

Programs during 1991 included Rabbi Zalman Schachter, healing, and focused meditation. The center staff organizes retreats with its spiritual leader, Baba Hari Dass, who has observed a vow of silence for 36 years and communicates by writing on a slate. It seems fitting that this outstanding community has a leader vowed to silence—what a pleasure to see how clearly silence speaks.

Mount Madonna Center
445 Summit Rd.
Watsonville, CA 95076
(408) 847-0406 or 722-7175

Accommodations: *For men, women, and children, everything from private rooms with baths to comfortable and pleasant dorms and tents; breakfast, vegetarian dinner, and a snack with produce from the center's own gardens served daily; completely nonsectarian, with programs including yoga, Judaism, Catholic mysticism, Sufism; private day and boarding school from preschool through high school with emphasis on the arts, community service, and positive values for staff children and children from local communities; full-time staff for a series of ongoing programs (including work/ retreat programs); 355 mountaintop acres adjoining forest preserve with hiking trails, volleyball, tennis, basketball, small lake for swimming; nice library; general store; oil massages and herbal steam baths available by appointment at additional charge; open year-round; private room $60 a day; double $45; triple $40; dorm $35; center tent $25; own tent $20.*

Directions: *Hwy. 1 to Watsonville, Airport Blvd. exit; go approximately 3 miles on Airport Blvd., then left on Hwy. 152 East. At the top of the mountain turn left into Mt. Madonna County Park (Pole Line Rd.). Follow the yellow line through the park and continue onto Summit Rd. The center is 1½ miles after park, on the left. From Hwy. 101 take Hwy. 152 West at Gilroy. Go approximately 10 miles through Gilroy and up mountain. Turn right at top of mountain into Mt. Madonna County Park and follow as above.*

New Camaldoli Hermitage
Big Sur, CA

The hermitage is located 1,300 feet above the sea in a remote area of the Santa Lucia Mountains overlooking Route 1, the two-lane scenic road that traces the California coastline. This 800-acre monastery affords inspirational views of the ribbons of surf below. The ever-changing weather of the Big Sur region is more pronounced here. On those glorious days when the sky is clear, the sea is a startling blue.

In 1958 three Benedictine monks came from Camaldoli in Italy, found the property, and built a monastery based on the contemplative and eremitical life-style espoused by their founder, St. Romuald: "Sit in your cell as in paradise. Put the whole world behind you and forget it. Watch your thoughts like a good fisherman watching for fish."

The Camaldolesi monks live here as a community of hermits and have their own cells in a private enclosure. They congregate in the chapel four times a day to sing the liturgy (5:45 A.M. Vigils, 7 A.M. Lauds, mass at 11 or 11:30 A.M., and Vespers at 5 or 6 P.M.). Guests are always welcome. There is a powerful silent meditation period following Vespers in the church rotunda.

There are nine single hermitages in a guest building at the end of the monastery road. Each room has a bed, table and chair, a bathroom, and garden with a view looking west to the sea. Food is brought to a separate pantry at mealtimes. Guests help themselves to the simple, hearty soups and salads accompanied by freshly made bread. Retreatants eat alone in their rooms and are responsible for keeping plates and utensils clean. Individuals structure their own time, but a monk is available on request.

The monks are known for their Hermitage Cakes, which they sell by mail order. The fruitcake and date-nut cakes are dipped in brandy and have a very distinctive flavor. There is an excellent bookstore, which also carries a selection of chalcedony art pieces created by the monks.

The outstanding setting of this remote spiritual outpost attracts many. The rooms are regularly booked so plan far ahead.

New Camaldoli Hermitage
Big Sur, CA 93920
(408) 667-2456 or 667-2341

Accommodations: *9 hermitages with baths and private gardens overlooking the sea from the top of this mountain; 2 trailers—one for men and one for women who wish to stay a longer time; 2 small houses for families, and 2 or 3 cells for men in the monastery itself; simple vegetarian meals with homemade bread are left in the guest kitchen to be picked up and eaten in your hermitage; dine with community on Sunday; Eucharist and 3 prayers daily for those who wish, with a ½-hour meditation following Vespers in the evening; 800 mountaintop acres in a wonderful natural setting overlooking the Pacific, with changing vistas of sea and sky, fog and mountains, adding to the experience; ecumenical; excellent book and gift shop; open year-round; suggested offering: $30 a day (reserve far in advance).*

Directions: *Located on Hwy. 1, 55 miles south of Monterey and ½ mile south of Lucia. Watch for cross on left and follow winding road to top of mountain.*

Nyingma Institute
Berkeley, CA

Almost at the crest of "Holy Hill," at the northern edge of the University of California at Berkeley campus, where every religious persuasion seems to have a building or an office, Tibetan Buddhist Tarthang Tulku was able to purchase an old fraternity house in 1973. The large but compact house has 25 residential rooms and space for up to 20 guests. Private retreats are available for those who have already attended a weekend workshop. From the entrance porch and the front windows, San Francisco Bay appears like a mirage on the horizon.

The great walls of the building protect the meditation-sitting room on the lower level against any outside noise or distraction. Seven prayer wheels spin here continuously, as do those on the front porch and a seven-ton prayer wheel in the backyard. These revolving copper drums are etched with mantras and filled with prayers and mantras written on paper; as the drums spin, the prayers are sent forth into the world. These are the only electric prayer wheels known—an American version of this ancient tradition.

Tarthang Tulku was one of the first Tibetans to arrive in this country in the late 1960s. A brilliant scholar and teacher of the Nyingma, or "Old Ones," school of Tibetan Buddhism, he engaged many Western psychologists in discussion and exploration of Tibetan Buddhist meditation and other practices.

There are classes (some for college credit), programs, workshops, and retreats given throughout the year on Buddhist teachings, Tibetan language, meditation, and psychology. There is a demanding nine-month work/study program during which the student is involved six days a week,

12 hours a day, plus some evenings and weekends. The work includes creating sacred art, maintaining institute facilities, and producing Dharma Publishing books and reproductions. Tarthang Tulku's teaching emphasizes directing energy to contribute something of value, developing skills to improve the quality of life, and recognizing limiting patterns in action and learning to break them.

Dharma Publishing, a major publisher of books on Tibetan Buddhism, was conceived when thousands of Tibetans fled their homeland and brought with them precious texts of their lineage. Tarthang Tulku found the means and ways to preserve the ancient texts by translating them for the West. There is an outstanding four-color catalog that lists these high-quality publications and reproductions of sacred art.

Nyingma Institute
1815 Highland Pl.
Berkeley, CA 94709
(510) 843-6812

Accommodations: *The institute has 25 residential rooms for men and women, each with 3–4 beds; about 20 guests can join the community overnight; mainly vegetarian meals in dining room; all retreats and workshops have practice as a component, and the community meditates daily at 6 A.M.; integrating study and practice is their aim; workshops, work/study programs, classes, retreats, artistic projects are all a part of the challenge to grow; garden with lovely prayer wheel; open year-round; $85 a weekend, $350 a week.*

Directions: *Rte. 101 to Bay Bridge, stay left and watch for signs to Berkeley. Take University Ave. exit. Follow University to end and turn left on Oxford; take first right onto Hearst and go 1 block past second stoplight to Highland Pl. Turn left 1 block to 1815 on right.*

Orr Hot Springs
Ukiah, CA

This remote retreat is named after Samuel Orr, who brought his family to the West in a covered wagon so he could prospect for gold in 1850. Eventually he acquired considerable land and settled in the mountains west of Ukiah to raise cattle and sheep. To utilize the hot springs found on his property, he built a bathhouse and a hotel with rooms for a dozen people, and opened for business in the late 1850s. The modest resort remained in the Orr family until the early 1970s. It is now owned by a cooperative of people who run and maintain it in a delightful way.

The winding two-lane road to the retreat is an adventure in California mountain driving, over the historic low gap road, which was built from Ukiah along an old Indian trail. Pomo Indians passed through the hot springs on annual trading expeditions and all tribes agreed to coexist peacefully while stopping here. It was a rest stop for the Ukiah–Mendocino stagecoach line and a popular resort for those seeking health and relaxation. A story from a 1906 publication described the waters as making "the skin feel like velvet . . . the hair soft and glossy, and the joints lose their stiffness like magic."

The guest cabins around the grounds, constructed in the 1940s from locally milled redwood, are in remarkably good condition. The bathhouse built in 1863 still stands near the hot springs where four porcelain Victorian tubs in private rooms are filled with mineral water at body temperature, then drained after use and refilled for the next person. A large wooden tub, filled with hot mineral water, can be used by five or six people at the same time. There is a large swimming pool built into the hillside, with cool mineral water, that is easy to plunge into after a hot bath or sauna.

Guests can choose from a private redwood cabin, a group sleeping loft, or tent sites for camping. Except for the private cabins, guests bring their own sleeping bags. All visitors should bring their own food, which can be prepared in the large community kitchen complete with cooking utensils and tableware, and eaten in the adjacent dining room. Refrigerator space and dry storage space are assigned.

The extraordinary care taken with the property demonstrates the resident community's great love for the place. The pathways have colorful borders of flowers and utility boxes are painted with elegant murals. There is no religious affiliation here, but anyone who wants to observe silence can wear a necklace of red beads. These are obtained at the main desk.

The sign near the entrance reads CLOTHING OPTIONAL ESTABLISHMENT ... YOU MAY ENCOUNTER NUDITY BEYOND THIS POINT; but you'll also encounter a respect for nature and for quiet.

Orr Hot Springs
13201 Orr Springs Rd.
Ukiah, CA 75482
(707) 462-6277

Accommodations: *For men, women, and children, 13 private cabins, simple but very nice, with down quilts, woven area rugs, queen or twin beds, private bathrooms, views of grassy mountains or the charming gardens; one cabin is a grass-roofed yurt; "The Vistas" (there are 3) have kitchens and woodstoves; also a dorm facility; large kitchen facilities where guests store and prepare their own food in a friendly atmosphere, and dine in comfortable lodge dining room; "silence beads" available if you wish to maintain a period of silence; quiet hours 10 P.M.–10 A.M.; clothing optional in 4 private porcelain hot mineral water tubs, the 8-foot redwood hot tub, swimming pool, and lounging pool; lodge with piano and classical instruments; massage available; hiking on trails, quiet road, Montgomery Redwoods State Park 1 mile away; open year-round; rates range from $20 a day (adult camping) to $110 a day (adult, "The Vistas").*

Directions: *Hwy. 101 North to Ukiah. Take N. State St. exit and turn right off exit ramp. Follow N. State St. ¼ mile north and turn left onto Orr Springs Rd. Follow paved road 13½ miles and watch for sign on left.*

Presentation Center
Los Gatos, CA

About seven miles from the charming town of Los Gatos ("the cats"), following Bear Creek Road to an elevation of 1,400 feet, the 264 hilltop acres of the Presentation Center sit serenely in a campuslike setting. When the Catholic Sisters of the Presentation acquired the property in 1956, they used it as Presentation College for a number of years until it was developed into the current retreat and conference center. The main buildings are classified architecturally as Adobe Aztec (Southwestern Indian Aztec with a Spanish influence)—or nominally as Early California. But there is an old-world charm in the existing buildings, which housed the Montezuma Mountain School for Boys from 1911 to 1955. Montezuma alumni still hold annual reunions here and in 1990 restored the outdoor Redwood Theater, set in a grove of redwood trees.

The community of 11 sisters who live and work here are committed to Christian hospitality. The facilities are available to any kind of nonprofit group, religious or educational, and have a wide range of users from high school retreats to engaged couples encounter sessions, weekends for Spanish-speaking men and women, as well as AA meetings. Private retreatants are also welcome. There are two chapels, one in the convent and one in the main building. Morning liturgy and daily mass is celebrated in one or the other according to group needs.

There are beds for 114, including those in eight cottages around the grounds. Many of the cottages, former housing of the Montezuma staff, are charming and self-contained, some with a small kitchen and living room. Meals are served cafeteria-style in the centrally located dining room. The food is delicious.

Near the tennis courts and swimming pool there is a large pond, and the paths, walkways, and roads make it easy for pleasant walking. There are marked hiking trails for more rigorous walks on the property.

Presentation Center
19480 Bear Creek Rd.
Los Gatos, CA 95030
(408) 354-2346

Accommodations: *For men and women, 114 beds in 50 rooms and 8 cottages, some with kitchens, each accommodating 4–8 people; delicious, nutritious buffet meals; daily mass in convent on property; chapel in main building available for group use; swimming pool, tennis court, volleyball, nature trail, pond; open year-round; $45–$50 a day, longer stays less.*

Directions: *From Hwy. 17 take Bear Creek Rd. 2 miles up and turn left onto property at streetlight. From Santa Cruz, watch for left onto Bear Creek just after Alma Fire Station. From north, pass Los Gatos and turn right onto Bear Creek Rd. Turn carefully when leaving if you have to cross Hwy. 17 to go toward Los Gatos. It may be safer to go right and turn around at next exit. Center will mail excellent map.*

Prince of Peace Abbey
Oceanside, CA

As we waited in the dining room at Prince of Peace Abbey, the 83-year-old abbot scurried by us with a nod and disappeared through the kitchen door. Minutes later he reappeared pushing a cart laden with boxes of food, bread and bananas protruding from them. He swept by us into the lounge. We could see him deliver the cart to a man who had been sitting, hat in hand, on a sofa. His face brightened as the abbot approached. The man took the cart and wheeled it away. The abbot then turned and came back to us. He sat down and apologized for keeping us waiting, explaining that the man was out of work and had a family to feed. "Now," he said, "what can I do for you?"

This compassionate spirit is a hallmark of the abbey. For many years, Brother Benno, one of the monks, took a truck out to gather food and served meals to the hungry at what came to be called Brother Benno's Kitchen in Oceanside. Every week, the monks baked 500 loaves of bread for those meals. In 1991, they opened the Brother Benno Center, where, in addition to providing food and clothing as the kitchen had done, there is space for such things as shower facilities, a mail and message center, an employment office, a counseling program, and literacy classes. "People see the abbey trying to do good things," one monk explained, "so they contribute. The more we help, the more help we get."

The abbey was conceived in 1958 when a small group of Benedictine monks were invited by the local bishop to come west from St. Meinrad's Archabbey in Indiana. The bishop was eager to have the benefit of monastic prayers in his diocese. The monks located a 100-acre ranch but were staggered by the asking price. Undeterred and resolute, the prior buried a

St. Benedict medal on the grounds and left the problem in the hands of the Lord, who eventually delivered the ranch to the young community for some $55,000 less than the original asking price. The abbey grounds are on a hilltop looking west to Oceanside and the Pacific Ocean and south and east to the San Luis Valley. There is a local airport in the valley, and planes take off into the prevailing western wind and fly by at eye level, but far enough away so there is no intrusive noise.

At the monastery, there are single and double rooms available for retreatants in a large building with a lounge and dining room. Three meals a day are served cafeteria-style, and friends of the monastery often drop by to eat there. The magnificent chapel nearby, completed in 1987, has excellent acoustics, and the monks gather there six times a day to sing the liturgy; mass is celebrated daily at 11 A.M. and on Sunday mornings at 10:30. There are no formal retreats, but a monk can be available for discussion if needed.

Prince of Peace Abbey
650 Benet Hill Rd.
Oceanside, CA 92054
(619) 430-1305 or 430-1306

Accommodations: *10 plain and pleasant double rooms with private baths for men and women and 20 singles, some with private baths; cafeteria meals with homemade wheat bread (breakfast and lunch for 200 local people in need provided at Brother Benno's Center nearby); prayer 5 times daily plus mass in lovely chapel with beautiful voices; prayer walk, peaceful ocean view, large library; open year-round; donation depending on budget of guest.*

Directions: *Follow Rte. 5 North from San Diego for 45 miles to Oceanside exit, Mission Ave. Follow Mission east about 3 miles to Airport Rd. Turn left on Airport to little bridge and* PRINCE OF PEACE ABBEY *sign. Drive up winding hill to top.*

Quaker Center
Ben Lomond, CA

At the end of a steep and winding country road a mile up from Ben Lomond, the Quaker Center occupies 80 acres on the slopes of the Santa Cruz Mountains. It sits high among the redwoods and fir trees, where coastal fog drifts in to give needed moisture to the forest. In the early 1900s, much of the property had been cleared of all marketable timber. Then a family became interested in the apples from the trees the loggers overlooked and purchased the land. They hosted scouting groups in the 1940s and later on groups concerned with preserving the environment. In 1949, Lucile Manley donated much of the land to the Religious Society of Friends: "To be perpetually dedicated and used for the enjoyment, betterment, education, and welfare of mankind."

Starting over 300 years ago in England with Christian roots, Quakerism today encompasses a diversity of beliefs. Quakers—or Friends, as they are known—assemble in groups to worship silently until the spirit moves an individual to speak. They believe in "continuing revelation" and that God still speaks today. Thus worship takes the form of quietly waiting for God's word. Though there is no formal creed or doctrine, the "peace testimony" that violence in any form is wrong is universally Quaker.

The facilities of the center are made available to those who are sympathetic to Quaker values and beliefs. The center has hosted a wide variety of seminars and is available for weddings and memorial services. Churches come for weekend retreats and authors have held discussions and workshops here. One group examined the 1991 Mideast conflict and asked, "If Kuwait's chief export was broccoli, would the United States be there?" and concluded that to pray for peace while managing a war was hypocritical.

In addition to welcoming individuals and families, the center has buildings of various sizes available for groups. The lodge has 12 double rooms with community bathrooms; the more informal hostel can accommodate 28 in two bunkhouses dormitory-style. The facilities are spartan and tent sites are nearby. Visitors can either prepare their own food or have the center arrange it.

The Casa de Luz Meetinghouse is on a high point with windows facing the San Lorenzo River valley and the far mountains. Hiking is rigorous and the views are rewarding.

For more than 40 years now, the center has identified itself as a place where meetings and retreats can be held in keeping with the Quaker principles of simplicity, justice, peace, and respect for "that of God" in everyone.

Quaker Center
P.O. Box 686
Ben Lomond, CA 95005
(408) 336-8333

Accommodations: *For men, women, and children, 12 rooms with twin beds and floor pad for third person possible for a total of 38 in the lodge; the hostel is a bunkhouse for 28 with a kitchen and meeting room, plus tent sites; Sojourners Cottage for 1–4 people with kitchen, living room; people do their own cooking, or center can arrange for meals on contract basis with known local cooks; mainly vegetarian meals; meditation cottage; Casa de Luz, a glass-walled meeting facility overlooking treetops at highest point on property; 80 acres of redwoods, firs, ferns, marked hiking and nature trails; volleyball; guests responsible for cleanup after visit; monthly conference of interest to Friends and open to public; yearly weeklong Art and the Spirit workshop with several artists-in-residence; last week in August a Volunteer Workcamp, where guests pay for meals only and help with projects on property (possible at other times too); open year-round; $85 a weekend, including food, lodging, program for group; Sojourners Cottage $20–$25 a day.*

Directions: *10 miles north of Santa Cruz on Rte. 9 to Ben Lomond. Watch carefully for left turn on Hubbard Gulch Rd. (second street past Ben Lomond Hylton Motel and just before Alba Rd.) and drive to top of mountain.*

Rancho La Puerta
Tecate, Baja California, Mexico

Near the southwesternmost corner of the United States, the Baja is an area just across the Mexican border. There, outside Tecate, Rancho La Puerta sits in a valley surrounded by rock-strewn mountains. The most prominent, Mount Cuchuma, is one of the 14 energy vortex points in the world. This valley has long been recognized as a sacred place, a pathway connecting ocean and desert, and a center of trade and spirituality for the Mexican Indians. To Ed Szekely and his wife, Deborah, it seemed a perfect place to start a health camp in 1940 for those interested in simple, nutritious, home-grown food and exercise in the fresh mountain air away from the stress and pressure of everyday life. Szekely had studied and written about the early Christian sect of Essenes, who advocated a life linked to the land. The Essene School of Life, which started modestly in an adobe hut with no running water or electricity, was eventually renamed Rancho La Puerta, Ranch of the (Open) Door, after live oaks that arched across the entrance to the property. In the early days, guests such as Aldous Huxley brought their own tents. Over the years luxurious villas have been built with private terraces for sunbathing and enjoying the fine views.

The guest rooms and villas are a few minutes' walk from the centrally located dining room, where first-rate chefs prepare a variety of colorful, healthy food at each meal. And adjacent to the various gyms (six in all), there is a separate lounge where on the first day of a weeklong stay guests may begin an optional fast of almond milk and juices.

No private vehicles are permitted on the grounds. The wide and brick-paved paths are bordered with sage, rosemary, and parsley. Cactuses and palm trees thrive and add dimension to the local chaparral. More than 60 species of birds have been spotted in the winter season, and numerous hummingbirds dart in and about the flowering bushes.

The ranch has grown in physical size and reputation since its early days, when it attracted "health nuts" who explored the Essene philosophy of uniting body, mind, and spirit. This philosophy is still followed in many ways as guests exercise, eat properly, retire early, and awaken before sunrise to hike on sacred land—to what purpose? Perhaps to be better people overall, kinder to family, friends, and associates, more compassionate to those less fortunate, enjoying the blessings we have rather than grieving over not having more.

As one staff member said, "Many people come just to get away, not for the exercise programs but to get in touch with themselves." And it is a wonderful place for that—join a group or not, hike or not. It is a place of transformation. Here is a retreat devoted to health, a mecca for fitness where first the mind and body find harmony, then the spirit comes alive, awareness increases, and the meaning of life is clarified.

Rancho La Puerta
Tecate, Baja California, Mexico
Mailing address:
P.O. Box 2548
Escondido, CA 92025
(800) 443-7565 or (619) 744-4222

Accommodations: *Lovely villas, haciendas, and rancheros for 150 men, women, and children; delicious, creative, mainly vegetarian meals—with much produce from the ranch's gardens—(fish twice weekly) of 1,000 calories a day (you can request extra servings at any time); yoga, meditation, t'ai chi ch'uan, hikes up sacred Mt. Cuchuma, a daily "Inner Journey" class, an optional silent dinner, plus full spa spectrum of exercise, massage, swimming, sauna, 6 lighted tennis courts, 6 gyms, weight training, volleyball, and evening movies and guest programs; open year-round; $1,200–$1,900 a week depending on accommodation.*

Directions: *I-5 from San Diego to Rte. 94 turnoff. Drive east on Rte. 94 for 40 miles to Tecate turnoff, Rte. 188 to right. Follow 188 for 2 miles to international border (open 6 A.M.–midnight). Cross border and proceed to second stoplight opposite town plaza. Turn right and drive west for 3 miles to clearly marked RANCHO LA PUERTA sign on right. Arrangements can also be made for vans to pick up guests at the San Diego Airport.*

St. Andrew's Priory
Valyermo, CA

In 1955, at the foothills of the San Gabriel Mountains on 710 acres in the Antelope Valley, a group of Benedictine monks settled after they had been expelled from Communist China in 1952. The community of 17 priests and brothers gathers daily in the chapel. They answer the call of the hand-rung bell to sing the canonical hours beginning with 6 A.M. Vigils and ending with Compline at 8:30 P.M. The low-slung, ranch-design chapel is made entirely of wood, and the roads and paths are bordered by meandering stone walls. Striking designs and architectural features can be found throughout the monastery, both inside the buildings and on the grounds. In the chapel, there are two altars: one is made of stone and wood and sits in the center, and the other, to the side, is made of concrete and seems like a sculpture that focuses our concentration on a central eye. One section of the grounds is reminiscent of the Far East, with a Chinese pagoda and tea garden set around a pond; another section is a carefully tended lawn in a group of cottonwoods and pines.

Three meals a day are served buffet-style in the dining room, except the noon meal, when the monks bring soup to guests at their tables. This room has an entire glass wall (reinforced by angled struts) that offers a view of palm trees and desert chaparral. The guest wing has 17 double rooms with private baths. These double-entry rooms have floor-length sliding glass doors out to the desert. These rooms are available to groups or individual retreatants. The comfortable and spacious lounge, off the dining room, and the chapel are always open; coffee and tea are available at the snack area.

Mainly in the summer months, there is a series of workshops on themes such as the care of self and others, and sacred dance. An important part of the priory's year is the Fall Festival, a weekend celebration that attracts thousands of visitors to dance, drama, and musical events. Fresh farm produce and ethnic food are available.

In the ceramic studio, the monks produce beautiful works of art that can be purchased in the monastery gift shop and are available in many shops throughout the United States.

Outdoor stations of the cross follow a semicircular path through the desert. The monastery grounds offer fine walking with extended views of the valley and nearby mountains.

St. Andrew's Priory
31001 N. Valyermo Rd.
Valyermo, CA 93563
(805) 944-2178

Accommodations: *34 beds in doubles with private baths for men, women, and children; tasty, healthful variety at buffet meals in community dining room that also has changing exhibits of work of local artists; mass at noon daily plus prayer 4 times, chapel open 24 hours; 710 gardenlike acres at 3,600 feet, with hiking, pond, and tea garden, Prior's garden, apple orchards, library, tasteful lounge, lovely gift shop; ceramics shop; closed in September to prepare for annual Fall Festival the last weekend in September; $40–$45 weekdays, $90–$110 weekends; group rates.*

Directions: *From Los Angeles take Rte. 14 to Pearblossom Hwy. exit. From San Bernardino take Rte. 15 to 138 and proceed 30 miles to Pearblossom. Take Longview Rd. (Texaco at corner) to Avenue W. Valyermo Rd. and watch for priory sign. They will send map if you request it, which will make it easier to find in this somewhat complicated location.*

St. Clare's Retreat
Soquel, CA

In 1949, two sisters of the Franciscan Missionary Sisters of Our Lady of Sorrows who had been expelled by the Communists from their mission-convent in China, arrived by train at Pismo Beach, California. They were meant to disembark farther on, at San Luis Obispo, where a priest was waiting with a car. They looked out at the artichoke fields that surrounded them and laughed at their predicament. This was a small inconvenience compared to what they experienced in China, where they had been interned in a Japanese concentration camp—their mission had been bombed and strafed and they were forced to flee through miles of battlefield debris. They had come to the United States as an advance team of their community, deputized to go to California and find a new course for their lives. They were determined to get the community back on its feet.

The bishop of Monterey-Fresno had heard of their struggles and invited the sisters to his diocese. There was a very popular retreat house for men in San Juan Bautista, so it seemed a natural step to found one for women, and the sisters undertook the assignment. They located the Mountain View Ranch, a resort just seven miles east of Santa Cruz. The main building sat on a knoll that faced the valley below and looked over ridge after ridge of redwoods and pines. The locale seemed ideal. The sisters took possession of the 50-acre site in January 1950 and held the first retreat there that spring. The dance hall became the chapel and the bar was converted into the dining room. Over the years, they have added 67 rooms with 87 beds, about half with private bathrooms. The main buildings are connected by walkways. A large covered deck surrounds the chapel, which makes it ideal for sitting and looking across to the mountains. There is an unheated swimming pool on a lower terrace neatly planted with flowering bushes and citrus trees. Hiking trails go down to the creek bordering the property and up to Meditation Point, a high spot on the property.

There is a full schedule of weekend retreats throughout the year, many for women only. Some are given in Italian, Spanish, or Portuguese. Retreat topics cover AA and Al-Anon, and also focus on preparation for Easter and Christmas. Many retreats are silent, and private retreatants are welcome at any time. One sister noted, "People leave on cloud nine, as though the pressure has been lifted." With the genuine hospitality and graciousness of the devoted sisters, that is easy to understand.

St. Clare's Retreat
2381 Laurel Glen Rd.
Soquel, CA 95073
(408) 423-8093

Accommodations: *87 beds in 67 pleasant motel-type singles and doubles with private or shared baths on wooded hilltop; tasty buffet meals; 3 prayer services and mass daily in lovely chapel looking out to woods; 5 trails and a mountain road for hiking; nice deck overlooking swimming pool, lush gardens; 5½ miles from beach; open year-round except Thanksgiving, Christmas, Easter; $35 a day.*

Directions: *From Watsonville proceed north on Hwy. 1 toward Soquel. Exit at the* CAPITOLA/SOQUEL *sign and turn right onto Porter St., which becomes Old San Jose Rd. In 3 miles turn left at Casalegno's Country Store onto Laurel Glen Rd. After 2½ miles turn right into St. Clare's Retreat.*

St. Paul the Apostle Monastery
Palm Desert, CA

Originally built as an investment by the cowboy movie star William Boyd, who played Hopalong Cassidy, the bungalow apartment complex called Whispering Isle was advertised as a vacation lodge located in the "golf capital of the world." Just a few miles from Palm Springs, Palm Desert sits above a huge underground water reservoir that has turned the desert into a tropical playground. When the Episcopalian monks of the Society of St. Paul acquired the property in 1977, the center was the last building on the block. As local development continued apace, the monastery dug in as a spiritual haven within the growing desert community. The walled complex is perfectly suited for monastic life and solitude; the former bungalows have been turned into monastery living quarters and rooms for as many as 18 retreatants.

The monks came to San Diego County from Oregon and searched for ten months before settling here. They felt their ministry would be determined by the new location and, after moving in, retreat work became obvious. The monks worked as carpenters, electricians, and plumbers to modify the apartments into comfortable, clean, and attractive rooms. Wanting their guests to feel at home, they worked to establish a welcoming ambience so visitors would feel "nurtured but not smothered." Setting aside some monastic disciplines in order to be better hosts, the monks have created an environment where they are available. They wear no habits except during the daily Eucharist.

Prayer services are held three times a day in Our Lady of Solitude Chapel: 7:30 A.M. liturgy, mass at noon, and 6 P.M. evening prayer. Guests are welcome. There are two beautiful stained-glass windows in the chapel:

the Wolterstorff window commemorates the first bishop of the Episcopal Diocese of San Diego; the other is in loving memory of Natalie "Dolly" Sinatra, mother of Frank, who died in a desert plane crash.

There are 12 retreats a year for 12-step groups such as AA and Al-Anon. The monks volunteer at the nearby Betty Ford Clinic and host vestry conferences and groups who come with their own agenda. Their quarterly magazine, *St. Paul's Printer,* is sent to 10,000 subscribers. Private retreatants are encouraged and welcome.

St. Paul the Apostle Monastery
44-635 San Rafael Ave. (street address)
44-660 San Pablo Ave. (mailing address)
Palm Desert, CA 92260
(619) 568-2200

Accommodations: 14 beds in 12 singles and 2 doubles with hand-crocheted throws at foot of each bed for men, women, and children; 3 meals served family-style; daily mass; swimming pool, hot tub, library; open October–May; suggested donation: $40 a day; flat fee for groups.

Directions: I-10 to Palm Springs; Rte. 111 South to Palm Desert; turn left on San Pablo Ave. partway through town. Watch for blue and white EPISCOPAL CHURCH WELCOMES YOU sign on tall post marking the Paulist Center on the right about 2 blocks after you turn. Turn right on San Gorgonio and then left on San Rafael. Enter through gate at 44-635 San Rafael.

Santa Sabina Center
San Rafael, CA

Occupying a quiet corner of the 100-acre campus of Dominican College, the elegant building that houses the Santa Sabina retreat and conference center has many European monastic touches. The arched doorway leads into a dark-wood interior, through one tastefully furnished room after another, to an inner courtyard of grass, flowers, and an orange tree—an inner sanctum where quiet and peace prevail; chairs invite the visitor to sit and reflect to the soft murmur of the fountain. The chapel has tall, narrow windows set in the stucco walls—another special place for quiet and contemplation.

There is a community of six nuns who live here coordinating thematic weekly retreats, monthly days of prayer, and evening studies of Scripture and the works of Thomas Merton. There are seasonal concerts on Sunday afternoons in the chapel. Private retreats are available by appointment. A community prayer meeting takes place each day at 6:30 A.M. and retreatants are welcome. Masses are available on the college campus at three different locations; there is also a mass in Spanish at the nearby San Rafael Mission.

There are 60 beds in 37 rooms with community baths for groups that come with a spiritual purpose or to attend a directed retreat. The conference room can accommodate 100 persons. Individual retreatants usually bring their own food or can walk to the college dining room nearby.

Though traditionally Roman Catholic, the center is ecumenical in its philosophy and outreach. Open to the influences of East and West, the sisters believe in the true essence of Thomas Merton's writings. They offer a chance for people to see the artist in everyone, the monk in everyone, and to appreciate the natural beauty of the place itself.

One can wander the entire college campus or hike up a fire trail to a lookout called the "rim of the world," which looks out over the entire San Francisco Bay, a panorama of city, bridges, and the ocean beyond.

Santa Sabina Center
1520 Grand Ave.
San Rafael, CA 94901
(415) 457-7727

Accommodations: *60 beds in 37 rooms for men and women; meals can be arranged for groups, individual retreatants can do own cooking; weekend contemplative retreats; Thomas Berry and Thomas Merton monthly evenings; 100-acre college campus and hills overlooking bay for walking; a little Buddha garden open to east and west; charming, intimate, inner courtyard and garden (like Santa Sabina's inner cloister garden in Rome); closed 2 weeks at Christmas; $25–$35 a day for private retreat.*

Directions: *Rte. 101 to Central Rafael exit onto Irwin St.; right on Mission, left on Grand, right on Acacia to Magnolia to Santa Sabina Center (with steeple). No entrance on Grand Ave. itself. Center is on campus of Dominican College.*

Self-Realization Fellowship Retreat
Encinitas, CA

The Hermitage House and its surrounding property were given to the Indian-born teacher Paramahansa Yogananda in 1937 as a surprise gift when he returned to the United States from travels abroad. The benefactor, who was a devotee, intended the place as a personal retreat for Yogananda. But a year later, the guru turned it into an open house so all could enjoy its beauty and serenity. The 17-acre property sits on a 400-foot bluff overlooking the Pacific. There are places for meditation along the bluff and there is a path down to the beach. To the side of the hermitage and above the main retreat building are the meditation gardens and ponds filled with colorful carp; the grounds of this tropical paradise are maintained with meticulous and loving care. At night, the lights of La Jolla can be seen ten miles south.

In the study of the hermitage, Yogananda wrote his classic *Autobiography of a Yogi*. His private rooms are preserved as a shrine where visitors are welcome Sundays from 2 to 5 P.M. The rest of the hermitage is now a residence for monastics of the Self-Realization Fellowship, who manage the property and run the regular retreat and education programs.

There are 20 rooms for retreatants and visitors in a building with a courtyard maintained with the same extraordinary care as the grounds. The food is vegetarian. The programs include structured meditation and classes on the teachings of Yogananda. Retreatants are expected to observe silence.

The rooms are usually filled by Self-Realization Fellowship members, one of whom said, "We all pass sooner or later between the beast and the saint, as different avatars come back. Here, we examine our attitudes and behavior and gently turn toward universal laws anchoring ourselves to that which is changeless—the *Bhagavad Gita* and the Bible."

Yogananda himself once said, "Every person needs a retreat, a dynamo of silence, where one can go for the exclusive purpose of being recharged by the Infinite."

Self-Realization Fellowship Retreat
215 K St.
Encinitas, CA 92024
(619) 753-1811

Accommodations: *20 single rooms for men and women; nutritious vegetarian meals; silence oberved in retreat enclosure; Thursday evening and Sunday morning lecture at temple; all meditations and public services end with prayers for world peace; classes in the teachings of Paramahansa Yogananda on meditation, reincarnation, health, energization led by nuns and monks of Self-Realization Fellowship; 2 meditation periods and 1 class scheduled daily; beautiful flower gardens overlooking Pacific maintained by postulant monks and open to public Tuesday–Sunday from 9 A.M.–5 P.M.; open year-round; suggested donation: $50 a day, $60 a day during conducted weekend retreat programs.*

Directions: *I-5 to Encinitas (24 miles north of San Diego). Exit on Encinitas Blvd. and go west to First St.; turn left and proceed through Encinitas to K St.; turn right 1 block to the center.*

Shasta Abbey
Mount Shasta, CA

In the very northern reaches of California near the foot of Mount Shasta, where the huge mountain's visage is often shrouded in mist and fog, a group of Soto Zen Buddhists came in 1970 to found Shasta Abbey. The monastery occupies 20 acres of forested land a few miles from town. The first community members moved into the abandoned motel without any electricity, gas, or phone. One winter morning, they awoke to find that seven feet of snow had fallen and they were completely isolated. For two weeks they subsisted on carrot-and-onion soup—the only food they had— until outside help could reach them. Since those early days, an entire complex has been built among the tall pines where a thriving community of 35 monks live. Covered outdoor passageways lead from the dining room to the subdued meditation room, where there are magnificent Buddha statues and shrines. The community follows a rigorous schedule beginning at 5:55 A.M. with zazen, meals, and work throughout the day till 10 P.M. Unlike any other Buddhist abbey, the morning and evening office is sung in English in four-part harmony, like Gregorian chant, with organ accompaniment.

The abbey was founded by Rev. Master Jiyu-Kennett, an Englishwoman who studied Soto Zen Buddhism in Japan and came to the United States following her master's wish that she transmit the teachings to the West. She is the author of several well-known books on Buddhism, including *Zen's Eternal Life* and *The Wild, White Goose* in two volumes— diaries of her years in Japan.

Shasta Abbey is the headquarters of Buddhist Contemplatives in the Soto Zen school and was founded as a seminary. Kennett-roshi describes the differences between Buddhism and Christianity thus: "There is no savior in Buddhism. You have to do it yourself. No one else will meditate for you. At the time of death you will judge yourself. . . . The ability to die in peace means the ability to live in peace. . . . We make our own hell. The only judging that is done is done by ourselves, thus hiding ourselves from the Cosmic Buddha. Everyone possesses Buddha nature—or, as Christians call it, the soul. It is hidden from our view because of our opinion of ourselves. The art of meditation removes that separation so we can return to our basic nature and truly know it. Meditation has nothing whatever to do with self-improvement. . . . Its purpose is to become one with the Cosmic Buddha, or have an experience of God."

There are guest rooms for 20 singles or 50 sharing. The rooms are clean and efficient. The food is vegetarian. There are retreats throughout the year from two days to two weeks, and many traditional Buddhist festival ceremonies are celebrated. This is a serious, sincere community, helpful and caring. Guests are expected to stay on the grounds during their visit. As a monk said, "There is always a schedule to follow. Be willing to stay where you are and concentrate on this specific approach while you're here."

Shasta Abbey
P.O. Box 199
Mount Shasta, CA 96067
(916) 926-4208

Accommodations: *For men and women, 20 singles, and up to 50 can be accommodated in shared space; vegetarian meals with dairy served in dining room; recommended that first-time visitors come for an introductory or weeklong retreat, then other options for retreats and visits available; limit your practice to their teaching while here; work is part of daily schedule; closed Christmas, New Year's, and 2 weeks for monks' retreats during year; $70 introductory retreat Friday–Sunday; $85 a week, $300 a month; reduced rates for longer visits.*

Directions: *293 miles north of San Francisco, 3 miles north of Mount Shasta on I-5 to Abrams Lake Rd. exit. Turn west on Abrams Lake Rd. over highway and make first right onto Summit Dr. ½ mile on right are 3 gates marked SHASTA ABBEY; go to northernmost gate, marked VISITORS' ENTRANCE.*

Shenoa Retreat Center
Philo, CA

The 160 acres of Shenoa is bounded on three sides by the Navarro River and adjoins the 800 acres of Hendy Woods State Park. In the dry season, visitors drive across the riverbed on a makeshift bridge; in the winter and early spring, the river reclaims its territory and cars are parked near the river. The only way to cross is via a swaying footbridge above rushing waters, and you wonder if this is *The Bridge of San Luis Rey*. Normally a truck meets guests, but the walk is less than a mile across a beautiful meadow to the isolated retreat.

The community seeks to provide a center for renewal, education, and service dedicated to the positive transformation of the world. In the tradition of the Findhorn Foundation in Scotland, members work to preserve and sustain a natural environment in which the healing powers of nature can be fully experienced. "World transformation," one member points out, "is something that anyone can be involved in, anywhere. We need only to ask: Am I being a way? Am I simply being a satellite in orbit around fixed ideas, or a new sun giving forth my own light of revelation? What am I doing to transform myself and my world?"

There is a regular program of retreats and workshops led by well-known facilitators such as Hal Stone and Sidra Winkelman, Ram Dass, and Pir Vilayat Khan. The courses and groups are diverse: Voice Dialogue Program, a Course in Miracles, Creating Our Future (a camp for teenagers), and a gathering of the West Coast Sufis. There are Elderhostel weeks in the autumn.

Guests are accommodated in rustic cabins that are simple but comfortable. Meals are served in the central lodge for gatherings or weekend programs. Otherwise individuals should bring their own food. Private retreatants are welcome but should expect to manage their own time. Camping is encouraged and the open meadow near the river is perfect for that. There are miles of hiking trails throughout Shenoa and the adjoining lands of Hendy Woods State Park.

The name Shenoa is derived from a Native American word meaning "white dove," a symbol of peace, especially the serenity experienced in nature. There is a spiritual approach here not associated with any particular ritual or religious tradition. "If anything," one community member said, "we err on the side of flexibility. We are no different from anyone trying to live a good life. Whatever others do is valid. So come to visit and be renewed, and go back and do good things. Pick up the consciousness here and use it to reenter the outside world better, not to escape from it."

Shenoa Retreat Center
P.O. Box 43
Philo, CA 95466
(707) 895-3156

Accommodations: For men, women, and children, a maximum of 55 beds in 17 nice cabins (homemade quilts) and camping for 50; delicious vegetarian meals; simple, open-air sanctuary available for meditation and quiet; open to all denominations; pool, hiking, organic gardens, tennis courts, badminton, baseball, 800-acre Hendy Woods State Park adjoins Shenoa's 160 acres; property surrounded by Navarro River; work exchange program, Elderhostels; open May–Thanksgiving, then suspension bridge access only, with special family celebrations at major holidays; $50–$55 a day with meals; $28 a day camping, with meals; special rates for groups of 20 or more.

Directions: Shenoa is 2½ hours north of San Francisco. Take Hwy. 101 through Cloverdale. Past Cloverdale turn west (left) onto Hwy. 128. Take Hwy. 128 for 30 miles through Booneville, and 5 miles more into Philo. Turn left onto Ray's Rd. and proceed ³⁄₁₀ of a mile to a fork in road; take left fork (gravel road) and avoid any residential driveways. Shenoa is 1 mile beyond fork, following this road as it curves down to and across the Navarro River, then meanders up the hill to the Shenoa sign.

Silver Penny Farm
Petaluma, CA

On the outskirts of the charming town of Petaluma, once known as the Chicken Capital of the World, the Silver Penny Farm is to be found at the foot of an almost treeless range of rolling hills that are dotted with grazing sheep and cattle. The 17-acre farm was given to the Archdiocese of San Francisco in 1986 by the Hearst family with the stipulation that the name not be changed since *Silver Pennies* was the title of the Hearst children's favorite book of poetry.

The main house, built in 1899, is a rambling, commodious building with a large living room with a fireplace where mass is usually celebrated. There is room for 24 overnight guests in the house, the nearby cottage, and the converted water tower. The cottage has a full kitchen where visitors can fend for themselves. This is a "do-it-yourself" center where the resident priest and one sister maintain an ambience of hospitality with part-time help but need and appreciate the cooperation of guests. Meals can be arranged according to group or individual needs. Bed linens and kitchenware are provided, but bring your own towels. There are a pool, hot tub, and sauna off the patio, and outdoor cooking is possible.

There are two separate meeting rooms: the Wagon House, for up to 60; and the Wagonita (Little Wagon House), suitable for about 8.

The farm, which is situated on a side road, is surrounded by open fields with abundant bird life, and one can roam, wander, or simply sit and enjoy the countryside. It is open "to those who seek God with a sincere heart." The stewards help to make the journey into the present moment a clear and delightful one.

This unobtrusive gathering place in the quiet hills of Sonoma County is serving a true need: there are more than 5,000 visitors a year. Weekends are generally fully booked by groups with their own programs, but space is usually available during the week, and private retreatants are welcome.

Climbing the hills behind the farm, one can look south for miles across the broad valley with neighboring farms and fences and see the meandering Petaluma River and the coastal mountain range in the distance.

Silver Penny Farm
5215 Old Lakeville Rd. #1
Petaluma, CA 94954
(707) 762-1498

Accommodations: *Comfortable and homelike rooms for men and women (and children at certain times); farmhouse—8 rooms (7 twins, 1 king), kitchen; the Tower—twins, sofa bed, kitchenette; the Cottage—3 twin-bedded rooms, kitchen, living room; the Wagon House—meeting room for 60; meals can be arranged for groups; mass at 4:30 Saturdays and on request; 17 acres, adjoining 300-acre sheep-grazing land and countryside for walking; swimming pool, spa, good library of video and audio tapes of spiritual leaders; fireplace, abundant bird life; open year-round; costs vary according to number in group, but average is $15–$24 a day.*

Directions: *45 minutes from the Golden Gate Bridge on Rte. 101 to Rte. 37, right for 8 miles to first stoplight and left onto Lakeville Rd.; then 5½ miles to Old Lakeville Rd. #1 (not 2 or 3). Second house on right—watch for sign.*

Sonoma Mountain Zen Center
Santa Rosa, CA

Set on 80 sloping, hilltop acres that look over the Valley of the Moon, where Jack London lived, the charming buildings of the Sonoma Mountain Zen Center sit unobtrusively in this quiet section of Sonoma County. The views across the valley are ever-changing in the mists that drift slowly in and out, then sharply clear on bright, sunny days—a natural metaphor for the condition of the mind during Zen practice.

In 1973–74, Jakusho Kwong-roshi with 7 students formed the center to continue the Soto Zen lineage of his teacher, Shunryu Suzuki-roshi. Suzuki was one of the few Buddhist priests in Japan to publicly oppose the rise of militarism prior to World War II. He regularly published warnings against aggressive military action. In 1959, Suzuki came to San Francisco and brought the stability of his Zen practice into the chaos of the Beat Generation, a voice of integrity in a society searching for values. Many Americans had abandoned their religious heritage because they felt the spirit behind the form was dead. Zen was attractive, a new form, and it felt alive. "But," as Kwong-roshi points out, "if you only perfect the form without getting the spirit, Zen is just as dead. When the spirit is alive you can see changes in people's lives and this is experienced outside the zendo."

There is a community of seven who live here, and other regular practitioners live nearby. There is a program of retreats throughout the year from three to seven days, as well as one-day sitting sessions and introductory workshops. There is a year-long resident training program and a month-long Ango Practice in July. The rigorous daily schedule begins with 5:15 A.M. sitting meditation, balanced by walking meditation, where each mindful, slow step around the sitting room, following the person in front, helps one to be aware of every sinew and muscle, every breath.

There are rustic cabins around the grounds for guests, who should bring their own sleeping bags. Heat is provided by woodstoves or electric heaters. There is a shared bathroom in the main building. Meals are taken with the community in the dining room.

The very available American-born Kwong-roshi encourages the friendliness and hospitality that are evident here. Kwong approaches Zen practice in a relaxed way: "The more you practice you realize it's not for gain but for gratitude. Gratitude becomes the biggest treasure, and practice is the way." Suzuki-roshi had said to him: "We are the same." Kwong explained, "He was telling me that the student and the master are the same . . . we are both Buddha!"

Sonoma Mountain Zen Center
Genjo-Ji
6367 Sonoma Mountain Rd.
Santa Rosa, CA 95404
(707) 545-8105

Accommodations: *5 cabins for men and women, with woodstove and/or electric heater; pick-up breakfast and lunch, prepared informal dinner with the community; daily zazen meditation begins at 5:15 A.M.; community day on Saturday with meditation, work-practice, meditation instruction, dharma talk, buffet lunch for those who have come for day; 80 acres of rolling hills and mountains overlooking Valley of the Moon; resident training program $385 a month, and special programs from 1 day, a weekend, a month; July–August practice is an opportunity for guests to experience a month of daily practice; closed last 2 weeks December; $25 a day solo retreat, $20 if practicing with community.*

Directions: *Take Hwy. 101 North past Petaluma to Old Redwood Hwy. and Penngrove exit. After 1½ miles turn right at small* PENNGROVE/SONOMA STATE UNIVERSITY *sign onto Petaluma Hill Rd. for 2½ miles; turn right on Roberts Rd. for 4 miles; at fork (red stop sign) turn right onto Sonoma Mountain Rd. and go 3 miles to large red sign on left and gravel parking area.*

Spiritual Ministry Center
San Diego, CA

In the mid-1980s, a group of Catholic sisters from the Religious of the Sacred Heart order discovered a perfect location to begin a spiritual ministry. At the time, San Diego, the sixth largest city in the United States, had no retreat facility. One of the fastest growing areas in the country, it is a military center and has urban sprawl of dimensions never before seen. The City of God was like a spiritual desert.

The local bishop encouraged the sisters to visit parishes and advertise their availability. By doing this they discovered an amazing hunger for spirituality. The response to their church programs doubled in size in the second year and grew sevenfold in the third. When it became necessary to find a permanent home, they located a two-story apartment house one block from the ocean in a quiet residential neighborhood. Here they live, hold retreats and prayer sessions, and have six rooms available for retreatants. The building was originally four separate apartments, and has been modified into duplexes for efficiency and comfort. The tastefully furnished private rooms with shared baths have all the comforts of home.

This "poustinia," where spiritual help is offered to those who seek it, serves as a welcoming community for people of all faiths and walks of life. The major goal is to help people discover, renew, and deepen their spiritual lives, and to find better ways to pray.

There are regularly scheduled programs dealing with mid-life crisis, the 12-step series and addictions, plus dream workshops, Meyers-Briggs, and the Enneagram. There is a two-year program to train others as spiritual directors. "The best measure," one sister noted, "is growth in love, however it manifests itself, usually by lack of self-concern. Once the self is in order, one can go on to help others."

This quiet place is just minutes from the ocean, where long walks breathing the sea air can clear the mind and heal the heart.

Spiritual Ministry Center
4822 Del Mar Ave.
San Diego, CA 92107
(619) 224-9444

Accommodations: *6 spacious, lovely, comfortable duplexes with private baths for men and women retreatants (4 can be used as doubles); there is even such attention to detail as umbrellas and flashlights with each room; fully stocked kitchen is available for meals; weekly mass at center, and many churches in area; nice library and reading room; bicycles; beach chairs and mats to take to ocean 1½ blocks away; little patio; massage therapist, acupuncturist available for a fee; silence is expected; open year-round; $40 a day.*

Directions: *Hwy. 8 West to end, exit bearing left onto Sunset Cliffs Blvd.; follow south for approximately 1 mile to Del Mar Ave. and turn right. Center is on right in first block.*

Tassajara Zen Mountain Center
Carmel Valley, CA

Deep in the coastal mountain range of central California, in the middle of Los Padres National Forest east of Monterey and up a torturous 14-mile dirt road that ascends more than 5,000 feet from Carmel Valley, the San Francisco Zen Center and its roshi, Shunryu Suzuki, established a monastic community in 1966. Closed to visitors during the winter for intensive Zen training periods, the remote retreat is open for guests from April to September. During this period, visitors join residents in sitting meditation, participate in programs and discussions, and attend lectures. The orientation is Zen Buddhist, which cultivates mindfulness to explore one's own nature and that of others, and awaken to and appreciate the natural beauty of life.

Formerly a resort where people came for the hot baths and seclusion, this area has changed little since the Esalen Indians used it for purification and healing. The baths are an integral part of community life. The hot spring area at the edge of a cold creek is divided so that men and women bathe separately; going from the hot tubs to the cold creek water is an invigorating experience. There are decks for sunning and relaxation. Tassajara is the Spanish word for "a place for drying meat."

The accommodations are spare but clean and comfortable. Some damage to the property took place during recent forest fires and the earthquake of 1989, but everything is gradually being restored. Rooms and pathways are lighted by kerosene lamps. Bring a flashlight and your own towel. Bedding is provided. The cuisine is vegetarian, abundant, and legendary. This is the home of Edward Espe Brown's *Tassajara Bread Book* and *Tassajara Cooking*. If there is a sensual side to the austere regimen of Zen, it is in eating. The food itself is a lesson in mindfulness as one looks at it, prepares it, consumes it, and thinks of its benefit, thanking the plants for giving us their energy and dedicating it for the good of others.

There are programs where participants can come for five days to two months and become fully integrated into the community through meditation, work, and study, or one can visit for just a few days.

The seclusion and peace, clean air, and magnificent views at Tassajara, the first mountain home of American Buddhist practice, have made it a popular refuge, so plan far in advance.

Tassajara Zen Mountain Center
39171 Tassajara Rd.
Carmel Valley, CA 93924
(415) 431-3771; for groups 431-9220, or write:
Tassajara Reservations, Zen Center, 300 Page St.,
San Francisco, CA 94102

Accommodations: Dorms, cabins, yurts, and suites available for men, women, and children guests with linens, blanket, and towels provided (bring a large extra towel for baths and an extra blanket in May); rustic housing for 2–4 and some family housing for work/study program participants, who must bring sleeping bags, towels, flashlight, and battery alarm since there is no electricity in their accommodations; for private guests rates range from $178 a night with private bath and deck to $65 for the dorm, minimum stay 2 nights; the work/study program costs $35 weekdays and $40 a day weekends, with a minimum stay of 3 nights; 3 delicious vegetarian meals included; daily meditation schedule, swimming pool, hot springs, hiking trails, classes, lectures, workshops, discussions; residency scholarship for work/practice program; 50 summer positions with stipends; open to visitors from late April to early September.

Directions: 5 hours south of San Francisco at end of 14-mile mountainous dirt road; arrange transportation through San Francisco office if you do not have a good standard transmission vehicle. Take Rte. 1 or Rte. 101 to Carmel Valley Rd. and follow to 23²/₁₀ mile marker (from Rte. 1) and Tassajara Rd. Follow Tassajara Rd. 14 miles to the center.

Taungpulu Kaba-Aye Monastery
Boulder Creek, CA

In a setting suitable for Buddhist monks following the Burmese forest traditions, the Taungpulu Kaba-Aye (World Peace) Monastery is located in a redwood forest in the Santa Cruz Mountains. Founded in 1981, the monastery consists of former school buildings that have been modified for the five monks and staff of four to provide simple living spaces and serve as a way station for others. It is a spiritual watering hole, where Theravadian Buddhists come for meditation, to practice, and to learn.

One monk explained, "The practice of the Burmese forest tradition is to go there to find quiet, solitude to meditate, away from distractions, a place difficult for visitors to reach. Thus, those who find their way are ready." He continued, "In Buddhism, we do not heal. We teach people to meditate well and by doing this they can accept their situation, or they can change their outlook and heal themselves. You must learn it yourself," he emphasized. "You must *do it yourself.*"

The orange-robed monks eat only one meal a day and sleep sitting up. They maintain silence as far as possible, which helps to develop spiritual strength. These ascetic practices are the keynotes of this tradition.

There are chanting and meditation sittings at 4 A.M. and sunset. On Saturdays, there is public meditation from 1 to 5 P.M. and visitors are welcome. There is simple, shared space for up to 45 persons with community baths. Visitors should bring sleeping bags.

On a knoll above the main buildings there is an authentic pagoda. Constructed in 1983, the Shwe Thein Daw Kaba-Aye Zedi (Peace Pagoda) is the only one of its kind in the Western hemisphere. The white circular shrine with a golden spear at the crown is shaped like an inverted top.

Beautifully crafted and maintained, it is carpeted inside and has many Buddhist paintings and statues. The trammel of the world is easily put aside in this holy space.

There are occasional weekend retreats and many Buddhist holidays are celebrated. Private retreatants are welcome.

The Very Venerable Hlaing Tet Sayadaw has been abbot since 1981 and a monk for most of his 80-plus years. Knowing that he had not been back to Burma for over ten years, a visitor asked if he missed his home. His robes flowed about his thin body and his face was the picture of benevolence as he replied through an interpreter: "All forests are the same."

Taungpulu Kaba-Aye Monastery
18335 Big Basin Way
Boulder Creek, CA 95006

Accommodations: *Extremely simple accommodations for men and women wishing to practice mindfulness meditation in the Theravada tradition under the direction of the abbot; 2-day group retreats for 35 people are offered 3 times a year; daily meditation with the sangha is at 4 A.M. and 6 P.M.; food offering to the monks is at 10:30 A.M.; meals for retreatants are vegetarian and nonvegetarian; suggested offering: $15 a day; open year-round; write for reservations and schedule.*

Directions: *Rte. 9 into Boulder Creek (which is about 20 miles north of Santa Cruz). At JOHNNIE'S SUPER sign turn onto Big Basin Way (Rte. 236) and drive 1 mile past the Boulder Creek Golf and Country Club. When you come to a 20-mile-per-hour hairpin turn you will see the monastery's carved wooden sign and the driveway on your left.*

Vedanta Retreat
Olema, CA

The 2,000 acres of the Vedanta Retreat are surrounded by the 62,000-acre Point Reyes National Seashore, a part of the California coast set aside to remain forever in its natural state. The drive is bordered by huge eucalyptus trees and leads to a sanctuary of meadows and woods. The Vedanta Society of Northern California, located in San Francisco, acquired this property in the mid-1940s. There are a dozen rooms: 4 for men in the meticulously refurbished main house, built in 1867; and 8 for women in a separate building in a nearby meadow. The rooms are comfortable and well furnished. Each guesthouse has its own meditation room. There is no formal retreat program. Visitors are asked to make sure that their personal practice does not interfere with others. Those who stay overnight should bring their own linens or a sleeping bag and bring and prepare their own food, cleaning up afterward.

Those interested in staying overnight or longer should arrange an interview with the swami in charge at the Vedanta Society headquarters in San Francisco. Day visitors are also welcome and can use the retreat from 10 A.M. to 5 P.M. with no reservations required. Spiritual seekers of any religious persuasion are welcome.

Vedanta means the end (*anta*) of the Vedas (ancient Sanskrit texts) or the culmination of spiritual knowledge. The basic teaching of Vedanta is that the essence of all beings and things, from grass to God, is spiritual, infinite and eternal, nonchanging and indivisible; that people in their true nature are divinely spiritual, one reality, one being. As is taught in the Upanishads, "Thou art That."

Swami Vivekananda, a chief disciple of Ramakrishna, brought Vedanta from India to the West in the 1890s. He taught that freedom can be attained "by work, or worship, or psychic control, or philosophy; by one or more or all of these." He emphasized three teachings as most appropriate and most needed by the modern world: a person's highest achievement and greatest happiness lie in fully manifesting one's own divinity; one's clearest vision lies in perceiving divinity everywhere; and one's truest worship is in selfless service to others, for they are in reality God.

Vedanta Retreat
P.O. Box 215
Olema, CA 94950
(415) 663-1258
(415) 922-2323 (for first-time overnight retreatants to arrange interview in San Francisco with swami in charge)

Accommodations: *Men's guesthouse—8 beds in 4 rooms; new women's center has 8 rooms they like to keep single, with private baths; bring your own food to cook; individual meditation (instruction available); "All sincere men and women spiritual retreatants of whatever religious persuasion are welcome to use the retreat house during the day for which no reservations are necessary, 10–5 daily"; walking on their 2,000 acres, surrounded by 62,000 acre Point Reyes National Seashore; libraries, meeting halls; open year-round; donations accepted.*

Directions: *1 hour north of San Francisco on Rte. 101 North to Corte Madera exit. Take Sir Francis Drake Blvd. West to Hwy. 1, turn south (left) for 2 long blocks and see sign on right.*

Villa Maria del Mar
Santa Cruz, CA

In 1891, the Catholic Ladies Aid Society of California accepted a gift of 20 acres of oceanfront land on Monterey Bay and built a three-story hotel where "women of limited means could spend a week recuperating from family cares, at little or no cost, and where nuns from teaching and nursing orders could afford to come in groups." Over the years, thousands have benefited from this altruistic attitude. The society rented half the rooms at prevailing resort rates to balance the costs of their charity. In 1963, the Sisters of the Holy Names took over the property and committed themselves to keeping Villa Maria a place where hospitality and family spirit prevail. There is an old-fashioned charm here as well as a sweeping view south to Carmel Point and north to Santa Cruz. The beach is easily accessible.

There are 20 rooms in the main house, and another 21 rooms in nearby Siena Hall and the Annex. The rooms are clean and comfortable, most with private baths. A large lobby with cozy places to read is next to the dining room, where the windows face the bay. The cafeteria-style meals are excellent.

Mass is said daily in Star of the Sea Chapel a few steps away. Built in 1906, the picturesque structure is a vestige of the past. Saturday evening mass is standing-room-only.

To maintain the spiritual mission of the villa, the community of sisters who live here host a regular schedule of retreats responding to the needs of today's Church. They are flexible to groups who have their own agenda. Private retreatants are also welcome. "Many who come are tired," one sister said. "They look out to the expanse of ocean, unwind, relax, and are healed."

Villa Maria del Mar
2-1918 E. Cliff Dr.
Santa Cruz, CA 95062
(408) 475-1236 (weekdays 9A.M.–noon)

Accommodations: *15 homey rooms in twins, and 5 singles, most with private baths, in the main house, many with view of Monterey Bay, just a few feet away; an additional 36 beds in 21 rooms in Siena Hall and the Annex; tasty buffet meals in dining room looking out to water; mass daily at Star of the Sea Chapel or the Villa Chapel across the way; swimming, surfing, fishing, state parks nearby, walking on beach, whale and seal watching; open year-round, though June, July, and part of August are predominately booked by sisters; $50 a day.*

Directions: *Hwy. 1 to 41st Ave. exit; 1½ miles south to E. Cliff Dr.; 1½ miles west on E. Cliff to 2-1918 E. Cliff Dr. on right.*

Wellspring Renewal Center
Philo, CA

This 50-acre retreat, with the Navarro River flowing through, is in the coastal hills of Mendocino County, adjacent to the redwood forests of Hendy Woods State Park. Down a quiet country road about a mile from Philo, this part of Anderson Valley is protected from inland heat by the mountains and the ocean, which is only 20 miles away. The buildings of Wellspring sit around a meadow regularly visited by quail and steller's and scrub jays. The place was known as Ray's Resort from 1923 to 1965. In the 1970s a group acquired it for the purpose of starting a retreat center that would have its own approach and personality. The programs offer ways of renewal and refreshment along life's journey. Weekend retreats focus on storytelling, the spiritual path, or pastoral approaches for addicts and their families, including gardening and outdoor activities such as canoeing and hiking. Every Memorial Day weekend there is a storytelling festival with workshops by well-known storytellers.

There is a wide range of guest facilities: a lodge for ten that includes a kitchen; cabins with electricity and indoor plumbing; more spartan cabins with kerosene lamps and a nearby bathhouse; a tent cabin; or the campground.

The central farmhouse, its distinctive wooden water tower under siege by woodpeckers, has a large, cozy central room used for dining and meetings and a well-equipped kitchen. The cooks are known for their skill in using local fruits, vegetables, and herbs fresh from the garden. Guests, particularly in the summer, are needed to help with garden care, harvesting, and collecting firewood. Individual retreatants, couples, and families should bring their own provisions and bedding (meals are provided only on special occasions).

There is no specific religious orientation, but the peace, quiet, and proximity to nature are truly refreshing. One guest wrote, "Most meaningful for me was a mid-morning meditation in the meadow. The wind blowing through the tall grass reminded me of the breath of the spirit. The redwoods were silent onlookers; the birds provided musical background."

Wellspring Renewal Center
P.O. Box 332
Philo, CA 95466
(707) 895-3893

Accommodations: *50 beds for men, women, and children in 2 lodges with double bedrooms and small kitchens; 3 cabins that sleep 3–5 with modern features; 4 rustic cabins that sleep 3–5; tepee and tent cabins that sleep 3 each, and a campground; meals (priced separately) are tastefully prepared using whole grains, fruits, vegetables from the center's orchards and gardens and served family-style (off-season guests prepare own meals or dine locally); volleyball, basketball, meadows, campfire pit, extensive hiking and bicycle trails into adjoining Hendy Woods State Park, swimming and rafting on Navarro River, which flows through the property; "Energy Gifts" of 1 hour a day work on property is asked of each guest; open year-round; $22 a day per person in lodges and cabins; rustic cabins $18 a day per person; tents and tepees $11 a person; campground $6 a person; 3 meals $20 a day (children half-price).*

Directions: *Wellspring is 2½ hours north of San Francisco. Take Hwy. 101 to left turn onto Hwy. 128 1 mile north of Cloverdale. Go 28 miles to Booneville and 5 miles more into Philo. Left on Ray's Rd. and follow 1 mile to end.*

White Lotus Foundation
Santa Barbara, CA

North of Santa Barbara up a steep road to the San Marcos Pass sits this mountain retreat center 1,600 feet above sea level. The center is built on the edge of a canyon and the views to the west and south of the city and ocean beyond are dramatic. The large main building is like a cave snug against the canyon wall, a secure vantage point from which to view the panorama of the seacoast and the Channel Islands far below.

There are two levels inside. The upper level is for meetings, reading, and dining; the lower section, airy, clean, and quiet, is used for yoga practice. Space is available for 24 guests with some in private rooms. Partway down the canyon there are four yurts (tentlike structures with a floor); each can sleep four adults. Guests use the facilities in the main building and also go there for vegetarian meals. There are hot tubs and outdoor showers as well as swimming at the canyon bottom, where the San Jose Creek flows year-round.

Weekend and weeklong programs, individual retreats, and workshops are offered, including daily yoga, music, dance, and discussions. A 16-day in-depth yoga training course is held three times a year that reestablishes rhythms, outlooks, and discipline and offers a personal transformation for the student.

Since the early 1980s, Yogiraj Ganga White has trained students at all levels of yoga. White is the creator of double yoga, a method in which two people practice together. He encourages students "to go beyond the limits of tradition and to follow their own path. . . . Everything we do at White Lotus is meant to empower individuals, not make them conform to dogma. We aim to awaken the fire of yoga within each student."

This is a very special location that allows spiritual seekers to experience new insights in a natural environment. Here visitors will find pure air, spring water, and hiking trails across 40 acres that have many secluded spots for reflection.

White Lotus Foundation
2529 San Marcos Pass Rd.
Santa Barbara, CA 93105
(805) 964-1944

Accommodations: *For 24 men, women, and children there are 4 yurts with 4 beds (showers and bath facilities in main building), 3 apartments for staff and guests, 8–10 beds in main building and 4 tents on this cliffside property overlooking the Pacific; vegetarian (usually organic) meals; regular weekday yoga classes; library; hiking down canyon to creek and waterfall; hot tub; massage; open year-round; personal retreats $35 a day, $60 with meals; programs priced separately.*

Directions: *Rte. 101 North to Cachuma Lake exit (Rte. 154). Follow Rte. 154 for 6 miles up mountain; watch for 2529 SAN MARCOS PASS sign on large white mailbox on left and turn into their private drive.*

Zen Mountain Center
Mountain Center, CA

In 1979, the Zen Center of Los Angeles purchased 160 acres of remote property high in the San Jacinto Mountains for use as a retreat. About 120 miles east of Los Angeles, the center is nestled in Apple Canyon, at the end of a mile-long dirt road, in a setting 5,500 feet above sea level. The clear mountain air and the pine, cedar, and oak trees make the center the antithesis of the City of the Angels. The life-style here is refreshingly simple: limited electricity is provided by solar conversion; central bathhouses have water heated by passive solar panels; and waste disposal units use a minimum of water. Guests should bring a sleeping bag, flashlight, warm comfortable clothing, and sturdy shoes. The temperature is generally 20 degrees cooler at this altitude than in the Los Angeles area.

The site still seems to carry the spiritual power of the Cahuilla Indians, who used to spend summers here to escape the desert heat. In the early 1980s, a monk who knew about homesteading and who was mindful of the locale helped to design and situate the buildings. A beautiful meditation hall made from unfinished wood and small cabins sit together in harmony within the steep canyon.

One corner of the the property lies on the Pacific Coast Trail, a popular route for experienced hikers. From a lookout near the trail, visitors can see the Pacific some 60 crow-fly miles away. Adventurous retreatants can hike six to ten hours to the tram that shuttles up and down from Palm Desert on the other side of the mountains. The view across the desert valley down to the green oasis of Palm Springs is spectacular.

A small community lives here, maintains the facility, and prepares for guests. There is a regular schedule of retreats throughout the year from weekends to the 90-day Ango, when the center is devoted exclusively to that. The Inward Bound retreat series, usually offered on weekends, is for professionals, teenagers, and all those interested in taking Zen to the workplace. As a monk explained, "All Zen practice—inward and outward, to self and to others—can be measured against the guidelines: You must help others; you should not harm others."

Zen Mountain Center
P.O. Box 43
Mountain Center, CA 92361
(714) 659-5272

Accommodations: Winter housing for 30 men, women, and children in private cabins, and summer housing for 50 with tents added; bring sleeping bags and flashlights since there is solar heat and light; bathhouses with hot showers and outhouses; predominately vegetarian meals depending on group; zazen twice daily and private instruction available; many interesting programs; Inward Bound, Zen for Health Professionals, Zen in the Workplace, Taiko drumming for children, Search for Self (for teenagers), t'ai chi ch'uan, plus regular program; late May through August is formal Zen practice and anyone is welcome to join; rest of year open for groups, private retreats, special programs; $50 per day, Zen Center of Los Angeles members $25 a day.

Directions: Rte. 74 East through Hemet about 45 minutes up into mountains; stay right on 74 at general store, left at Apple Canyon Rd.; large turnout, and fork, stay right on pavement; at Pine Springs Ranch gate take the dirt road in middle (a continuation of paved road) and continue on up to center.

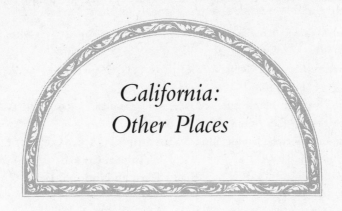

California:
Other Places

Sacred Heart Retreat Center, 920 E. Alhambra Rd., **Alhambra,** CA 91801. (818) 289-1359

Camp Sky Meadows, 3191 Radford Rd., **Angelus Oaks,** CA 92305. (714) 866-2268

Sacred Heart Retreat Camp, P.O. Box 1795, **Big Bear Lake,** CA 92315. (714) 866-5696

Commonweal Center, P.O. Box 316, **Bolinas,** CA 94924. (415) 868-9205

Vajrapani Institute, P.O. Box 1, **Boulder Creek,** CA 95006. (408) 338-6654

Rainbow Ranch, 3975 Mountain Home Rd., **Calistoga,** CA 94515. (707) 942-5127

St. Dorothy's Rest, Box B, **Camp Meeker,** CA 95419. (707) 874-3319

Notre Dame House of Prayer, 27951 Hwy. 1, **Carmel,** CA 93923. (408) 624-9416

Avery Ranch, P.O. Box 1186, **Columbia,** CA 95310. (209) 533-2851

Madonna of Peace Renewal Center, P.O. Box 71, **Copperopolis,** CA 95228. (209) 785-2157

San Damiano Retreat House, 710 Highland Dr., P.O. Box 767, **Danville,** CA 94526. (510) 837-9141

Sky Valley Retreat Center, 732 Dillon Rd., **Desert Hot Springs,** CA 92240. (619) 329-6994

Madre Grande Monastery, 18372 Hwy. 94, **Dulzura,** CA 91917. (619) 468-3810 and 468-3006

Holy Spirit Retreat Center, 4316 Lanai Rd., **Encino,** CA 91436. (818) 784-4515

Christ the Victor Lutheran Retreat, 2626 Sir Francis Drake Blvd., **Fairfax,** CA 94930. (415) 454-6365

Our Lady of Trust Spirituality Center, 205 S. Pine Dr., **Fullerton,** CA 92633. (714) 956-1020

Institute, 220 Harmony Lane, **Garberville,** CA 95440. (707) 923-

Ashram, Vrindavan Yoga Farm, 14651 Ballantree Ln. **Grass Valley,**
5949. (916) 272-9322

pring Mountain Retreat, P.O. Box 1335, **Hayfork,** CA 96041. (916)
628-4393 (messages)

Riverrun Retreat Hermitage, c/o Simon Jeremiah, 1569 Fitch Mountain,
Healdsburg, CA 95448. (707) 433-6754

St. Columba's Retreat House, Box K, **Inverness,** CA 94937. (415) 669-1039

Astral Mountain Retreat, Box 1881, Dept. YJ, **Julian,** CA 92036. (619) 765-1225

Far Horizons, Inc., P.O. Box 857, **Kings Canyon National Park,** CA 93633.
(209) 565-3692

Villa Maria House of Prayer, 1252 N. Citrus, **La Habra,** CA 90631. (310)
691-5838

Double D Ranch, 3212 E. 8th St., **Long Beach,** CA 98084. (310) 434-3453

Jesuit Retreat House, 300 Manresa Way, **Los Altos,** CA 94022. (415) 948-4491

Claretian Renewal Center, 1119 Westchester Pl., **Los Angeles,** CA 90019.
(213) 737-8464

Jikoji, 12100 Skyline Boulevard, **Los Gatos,** CA 95030. (408) 741-9562

Serra Retreat, P.O. Box 127, **Malibu,** CA 90265. (310) 456-6631

Ralston L. White Retreat, 2 El Capitan Ave., **Mill Valley,** CA 94941. (415)
388-0858

DePaul Center, 1105 Bluff Rd., **Montebello,** CA 90640. (213) 723-7343

Las Brisas Retreat Center, 43500 Camino de Las Brisas, **Murrieta,** CA 92562.
(714) 677-4544

The Expanding Light at Ananda, 14618 Tyler Foote Rd., **Nevada City,** CA
95959. (800) 346-5350

Episcopal Conference Center, P.O. Box 1355, **Oakhurst,** CA 93644. (209)
683-8162

Holy Redeemer Center, 8945 Golf Links Rd., P.O. Box 5427, **Oakland,** CA
94605. (510) 635-6341

Chagdud Gonpa Foundation Inc., P.O. Box 90, **Oakville,** CA 94562. (707)
944-1907

House of Prayer for Priests, 7734 Santiago Canyon Rd., **Orange,** CA 92669.
(714) 639-9740

Spiritual Development Center, 434 S. Batavia, **Orange,** CA 92668. (714) 744-
3175

Asilomar Conference Center, P.O. Box 537, **Pacific Grove,** CA 93950. (408)
372-8016

Woodside Priory, 302 Portola Road, **Portola Valley,** CA 94028. (415) 851-
8220

Dominguez Retreat Center, 18127 S. Alameda St., **Rancho Dominguez,** CA 90220. (213) 636-6030

Mary and Joseph Retreat Center, 5300 Crest Rd., **Rancho Palos Verdes,** CA 90274. (310) 377-4867

El Carmelo Retreat House, 926 E. Highland Ave., **Redlands,** CA 92373. (714) 792-1047

Mount Alverno Retreat Center, P.O. Box 1028, 3910 Bret Harte Dr., **Redwood City,** CA 94064. (415) 369-0798

Divine Word Retreat Center, 11316 Cypress Ave., **Riverside,** CA 92505. (714) 689-4858

Christian Brothers Retreat House, 2233 Sulphur Springs Ave., **St. Helena,** CA 94574. (707) 963-1411

Zen Center, 300 Page Street, **San Francisco,** CA 94102. (415) 863-3136

United Camps, Conferences, & Retreats, 199 Greenfield, **San Rafael,** CA 94901. (415) 456-5102

St. Mary's Retreat House, 505 E. Los Olivos, **Santa Barbara,** CA 93105. (805) 682-4117

San Lorenzo Friary, P.O. Box 247, 1802 Sky Dr., **Santa Ynez,** CA 93460. (805) 688-1993

Westerbeke Ranch & Conference Center, 2300 Grove St., **Sonoma,** CA 95476. (707) 996-7546

Land of Medicine Buddha, 5800 Prescott Rd., **Soquel,** CA 95073. (408) 462-8383.

City of 10,000 Buddhas, P.O. Box 217, **Talmadge,** CA 95481-0217. (707) 462-0939

St. Anthony Retreat Center, 43816 Sierra Dr., **Three Rivers,** CA 93271. (209) 561-4595

Saratoga Springs, 10243 Saratoga Springs Rd., **Upperlake,** CA 95485. (707) 275-9503.

St. Francis Salesian Retreat, 2400 E. Lake Ave., **Watsonville,** CA 95076. (408) 722-0115

Stewart Mineral Springs, 4617 Stewart Spring Rd., **Weed,** CA (916) 938-2222.

Our Lady of the Redwoods, **Whitethorn,** CA 94589. (707) 986-7419

Wilbur Hot Springs, Star Route, **Williams,** CA 95987. (916) 473-2306

Spirit Rock Center, P.O. Box 909, **Woodacre,** CA 94973. (415) 488-0164

Camp Mariastella, P.O. Box 99, **Wrightwood,** CA 92397. (213) 733-1208

Luther Glen Conference Center, 39136 Harris Rd., **Yucaipa,** CA 92399. (714) 797-9183

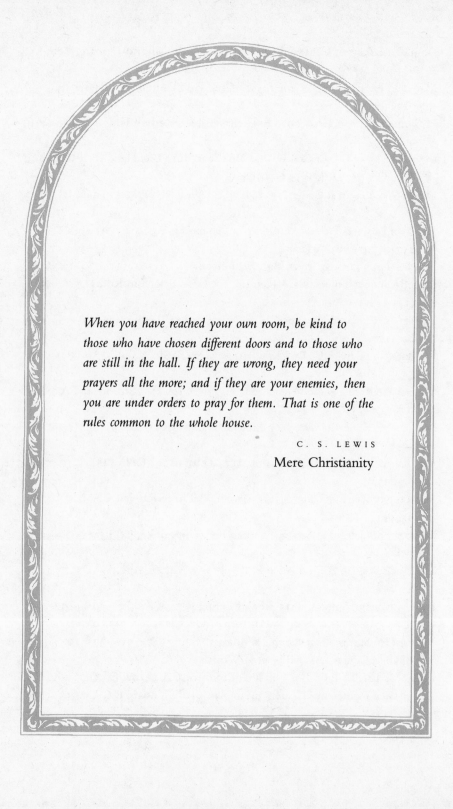

When you have reached your own room, be kind to those who have chosen different doors and to those who are still in the hall. If they are wrong, they need your prayers all the more; and if they are your enemies, then you are under orders to pray for them. That is one of the rules common to the whole house.

C. S. LEWIS
Mere Christianity

Colorado

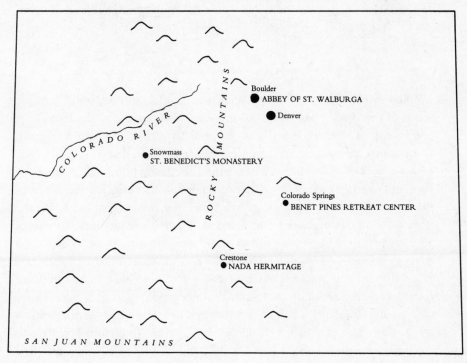

Boulder
● ABBEY OF ST. WALBURGA

● Denver

● Snowmass
ST. BENEDICT'S MONASTERY

Colorado Springs
● BENET PINES RETREAT CENTER

Crestone
● NADA HERMITAGE

COLORADO RIVER

ROCKY MOUNTAINS

SAN JUAN MOUNTAINS

Abbey of St. Walburga
Boulder, CO

In 1867 this 150 acres of valley land just outside Boulder, with dramatic views of the Rocky Mountains to the west, was bought by the first Catholic bishop of Denver. But it was not until 1935 that a successful religious community was established there when three German sisters fled from Nazi persecution and moved in. They repaired the leaky house and dilapidated barn and eked out a meager existence. Helpful neighbors lent farm equipment and showed them how to irrigate. They persevered and today the farm is a model of efficiency and neatness. The community now consists of 20 contemplative nuns who follow the Benedictine tradition. Their main purpose is the Divine Office. They gather seven times a day in the elegant brick chapel from 4:30 A.M. Matins to 8 P.M. Compline to sing the office to the accompaniment of an Aeolian Skinner pipe organ. In between, they raise 60 beef cattle plus llamas and sheep. They grow hay for the animals and tend a large garden for their own use, do weaving from llama wool, embroider vestments, bake bread, cook, and clean, yet all these activities revolve around the canonical hours.

Over the years, visitors have come in increasing numbers and the retreat facilities and programs have grown. There are now 45 weekend retreats each year. There are beds for 38 in singles, doubles, and some larger rooms. Private retreatants are accommodated as space permits. Spiritual direction is available for those who seek it. There is an oblate program of 30 students who meet regularly at the abbey for spiritual nourishment and follow the Benedictine Rule in their outside life.

As the abbess writes: "Contemplatives are like the pump hidden deep in the bottom of the well, close to the life-giving waters of God's love. They are channels through which God's love and grace overflow to a reservoir, for all who wish to draw from it."

Many do come to the well, to see the stability of life, to join in, or watch the sisters go purposefully about their chores, to hear the beautiful singing, and to find rest and renewal in a splendid mountain setting.

Abbey of St. Walburga
6717 S. Boulder Rd.
Boulder, CO 80303
(303) 494-5733

Accommodations: *Beds for 38 men, women, and children in singles, doubles, and triples in abbey and guesthouses (one with own kitchen); home-cooked meals served in dining room with view of Rockies; community meets 7 times a day for sung and chanted prayer, their own unique adaptation of Gregorian melodies (the abbess spent 4 years translating liturgy and compiling books so congregation can sing along); 150 acres; cattle, llamas, and other barnyard animals; much work available on the farm, in the fields, in the abbey and kitchen; open year-round; $30 for first day, $28 each day thereafter.*

Directions: *U.S. 36 to Boulder. Exit at Table Mesa Dr./S. Boulder Rd.; go east on S. Boulder Rd. for 2 miles and turn left into driveway, then left into abbey courtyard (if you go straight you go to parish).*

Benet Pines Retreat Center
Colorado Springs, CO

In 1965, the Catholic Benedictine sisters of Benet Hill Monastery bought 27 acres of hilltop land and ponderosa pine to use as a community retreat just north of Colorado Springs. Up a quiet country road, the property is at the crest of low hills with a dramatic view of Pike's Peak. From the picture window in the chapel in the main house, there is an extraordinary view of the mountains across the valley.

While initially using the haven for their own community, the sisters soon began to share the country setting to provide a place for people to "come away and rest a while." There are now three houses for up to 17 overnight guests, a 50-person conference hall, and three hermitages tucked away in the pines. Three sisters staff the center and organize days of prayer, spiritual direction, and directed retreats, and also hold daily centering prayer sessions. They welcome those interested to join them for a day or a longer period of time to suit personal needs. The community comes together three or four times a day, around mealtimes, to pray. Meals can be taken with the community or by oneself; some of the guesthouses have kitchen facilities. One recent Christmas, a family rented a cottage to get away from the commercial distractions of the holiday and spent a spiritual vacation, a delightful experience for the community and the family.

The sisters who live here follow a simple, monastic life-style in the character of Benedictines, who greet all visitors as though they were Christ. These hospitable, generous women make everyone feel at ease, and the peace of the place is almost tangible. One retreatant wrote, "It was possible to go outside, stand on the mountain, and listen for a whispering sound." The only sound one does hear in this secluded retreat is that of the wind sighing in the tall pines.

Benet Pines Retreat Center
15780 Hwy. 83
Colorado Springs, CO 80921
(719) 495-2574

Accommodations: *For men, women, and children, beds for 17 in 2 cottages and 3 hermitages scattered in the pines; delicious home-cooked meals with the community or in silence, 2 of the houses have kitchens; join the community for centering prayer and morning, noon, and evening praise; mini-sabbaticals available for 3 months to 1 year for quiet reflection and monastic rhythms of life; help in garden, forest, household; open year-round; suggested freewill offering: $30–$40 a day.*

Directions: *From Denver take I-25 South to Monument, exit to Hwy. 105 East to Hwy. 83—right 2⁸⁄₁₀ miles.*

Nada Hermitage
Crestone, CO

This community of hermits chose its location for solitude and natural grandeur. It is situated on the gently sloping eastern edge of the San Juan Valley, which is the largest alpine valley in North America—the size of the state of Delaware. The site looks west to the La Garita Mountains some 40 miles away. The community moved here in the early 1980s when its southern Arizona location was encroached on by development and the 180,000-acre Baca Ranch in southern Colorado was being divided and parcels donated to religious groups who would improve and live on the land. Nada is in the foothills of the Sangre de Cristos, where several mountains tower over 14,000 feet. Visible to the south is Sierra Blanco, the fourth highest peak in Colorado, one of four mountains sacred to the Hopi.

This youthful group of apostolic hermits, both men and women, was inspired by the teachings and writings of Father William McNamara, who had been deeply influenced by discussions with Thomas Merton in the 1950s. They live together but each has an individual hermitage and lives a life of solitude, with personal duties and responsibilities to community life. The schedule is a simple one: Vespers daily at 5 P.M.; Saturday Lauds at 6 A.M. On Saturday night there is an all-night vigil for peace before the Blessed Sacrament in the chapel, each person signing up to spend an hour during the night. On Sunday there is a sung mass at 9 A.M., followed by a community breakfast in Agape, the lovely main building, which houses a library, the dining room, the main kitchen, and food supplies. This is a happy, convivial occasion when guests and community members share social time. Often more than 20 people sit together at the large table with an interesting custom: only one person speaks at a time, thus all are able to follow the discussion.

Retreatants come for a week from Thursday afternoon to the following Wednesday at noon. A monk is available for spiritual direction if requested. The artfully designed and constructed adobe hermitages are heated by passive solar energy and a backup woodstove. Each has electricity, kitchen facilities and utensils, and a bathroom. The hermitages are set apart from each other and face south with a view to the valley and distant mountains. Bedding and food are provided, but each person sleeps when tired and eats when ready—alone.

The chapel is always open for prayer and reflection, the high ceilings over the altar balanced by tall windows looking out to the grand mountains. There is a significant sculpture of Christ crucified that seems to capture the essence of the suffering.

Standing alone in the quiet of that desert, looking at the vast, clear sky filled with stars and to the black outlines of the far-off mountains, one experiences the full power of solitude.

Nada Hermitage
Spiritual Life Institute
Crestone, CO 81131
(719) 256-4778

Accommodations: *Approximately 8 of the 17 hermitages (2 doubles) are available for men and women guests; a basic wilderness experience of solitude in lovely accommodations nestled around the desert property; extra touches like homemade quilts on beds; hermitage kitchens fully stocked with healthful food to make own meals; community gathers for breakfast with guests after Sunday mass; retreatants and community work together in afternoon before Friday evening mass and supper together; 100 desert acres surrounded by mountains and crisscrossed by hiking trails; cross-country skis available; stable nearby; work on property encouraged; open year-round; $45 first day, $35 each additional day for singles; $55 first day, $45 each additional day for double-occupancy.*

Directions: *Crestone is 1 hour north of Alamosa or 1 hour south of Salida on Colorado Hwy 17. By car it is 4 hours south of Denver and 5 hours north of Albuquerque. The Crestone turnoff from Hwy. 17 ("Road T") is just south of the town of Moffat. Go 12 miles toward Crestone. Just past a small church on the left is the entrance to Baca Grande. Continue 1½ miles and turn right onto Badger Rd. at the sign for the stables. Go ⁹⁄₁₀ mile down the hill and turn right onto Carmelite Way. Follow this curving road to end.*

St. Benedict's Monastery
Snowmass, CO

In 1956 a group of Trappist monks from Spencer, MA, chose this place deep in the Rocky Mountains as the site for their new foundation. Seven miles from the nearest village, in a valley more than 8,000 feet above sea level, it is surrounded by the craggy peaks of the majestic mountains that run north and south through the state of Colorado. One monk mused, "A monastery should be in a place that is hard to get to and difficult to leave." Traversing mountain passes on the way from Denver, one realizes the courage and tenacity necessary to build and live here. The daily drama of nature is awesome: The wind moves the snow on the distant mountain peaks, coyotes utter their mournful cries, an owl hoots in the still night air beneath the star-filled sky.

All the more striking are the somberly attired monks who assemble seven times each day in the stark, timeless chapel to sing the canonical hours. Guests are invited to sit along the walls just behind the monks' chairs, much closer than usual. Hymnals and prayer books are available for those who wish to join in the liturgy. On Thursday evening, mass is celebrated at a table, like the Last Supper. After the main service, the monks assemble in the foyer and chat amiably with retreatants: "We're glad you're here; thanks for making the effort." They see this as an extension of the service. The goodwill these men bring to visitors is wonderful to behold.

This is the home of Father Thomas Keating, the noted writer and proponent of centering prayer. The guestmaster is Father Theophane, author of *Tales of a Magic Monastery,* a gem of parables that has helped many on their spiritual search. The guesthouses, one a former farmhouse, have facilities for cooking, and visitors should bring and prepare their own food.

The guest facilities are some distance from the chapel, along a road used only for the monastery, and it is a pleasant walk to services. The 4,000 acres of monastery property offer plenty of space for hiking. In the winter, one can cross-country ski.

The monastery supports itself by ranching and baking and selling the popular Snowmass Monastery Cookies. When the monks began their cookie business some years ago, they called on Bernard Tetsugen Glassman, a Zen master in New York, who founded and still runs the Greyston Bakery, and he helped them get started.

There is a once-a-month intensive retreat often run by Father Keating. From time to time, groups will meet here, using this quiet, out-of-the-way spot to concentrate on their own spiritual program. Private retreatants can usually be accommodated for a few days or longer. There is even a six-month program for those interested in living with the community and learning the discipline of St. Benedict through "the bells and the eyes of the brethren."

St. Benedict's Monastery
1012 Monastery Rd.
Snowmass, CO 81654
(303) 927-3311

Accommodations: *For men and women, 11 beds in ranch house, guesthouse, and barn; bring food to cook at ranch and guesthouse; men can join community for lunch; meals provided for 10-day "intensives"; canonical hours with wonderful music and voices; monks meet with attendees after mass (an extension of mass); 4,000 acres for walking, biking, cross-country skiing; help working on farm and packing cookies; 6-month program for men; open year-round; freewill donation.*

Directions: *From Denver take Rte. I-70 to Glenwood Springs. Then follow Hwy. 82 from Glenwood Springs to Old Snowmass, which is 2½ miles past Basalt, CO. Watch for an intersection with a Conoco gas station on the right, and turn right there. Go straight for about 7½ miles (bearing right at the one crossroads) until you see a sign for the monastery on the left side of the road. Turn left at the sign. (If you run onto an unpaved road before making a left turn, you have missed the monastery road.) After you make the left, travel 1 mile to the gatehouse, which is next to a large wooden arch spanning the road.*

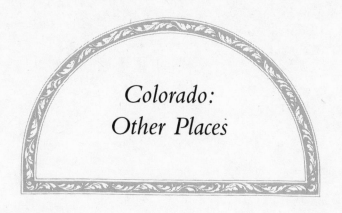

Colorado:
Other Places

St. Malo Center, 10758 Hwy. 7, **Allen's Park,** CO 80510. (303) 444-5177

Eldorado Mt. Yoga Ashram, 2875 County Rd. 67, **Boulder,** CO 80303. (303) 494-3051

Holy Cross Abbey, P.O. Box 1510, **Canon City,** CO 81215. (719) 275-8631

Benet Hill Center, 2577 N. Chelton Rd., **Colorado Springs,** CO 80909. (719) 473-6184

Franciscan Center, 7665 Assisi Heights, **Colorado Springs,** CO 80919. (719) 598-5486

Mercy Center, 926 Farragut Ave., **Colorado Springs,** CO 80909. (719) 633-2302

House of Spirit, 2202 Q50 Ln., **Cedaredge,** CO 81413. (303) 856-6626

Dharma Sangha, P.O. Box 130, **Crestone,** CO 81131.

Haidakhandi Universal Ashram, 184 Moonlight Overlook, P.O. Box 9, **Crestone,** CO 81131. (719) 256-4108

Queen of Peace Oratory, 5360 Columbine Rd., **Denver,** CO 80221. (303) 477-9139

Regis Retreat Center, 3333 Regis U. Blvd., **Denver,** CO 80221. (303) 458-4100

Estes Park Center, P.O. Box 20456, **Estes Park,** CO 80511. (303) 586-3341

Bethlehem Center, 12550 Zuni, **Northglen,** CO 80234. (303) 451-1371

Spirit Rest Retreat & Holistic Health Center, P.O. Box 1916, **Pagosa Springs,** CO 81147. (303) 264-2573

Rocky Mountain Dharma Center, 1921 County Rd. 68C, **Red Feather Lakes,** CO 80545. (303) 881-2184

Shoshoni Yoga Retreat, P.O. Box 410, **Rollinsville,** CO 80474. (303) 642-0116

Jesuit Retreat House, P.O. Box 185, **Sedalia,** CO 80135. (303) 688-4198

Whitewater Community, 8250 Kannah Creek Rd., **Whitewater,** CO 81527. (303) 241-3847

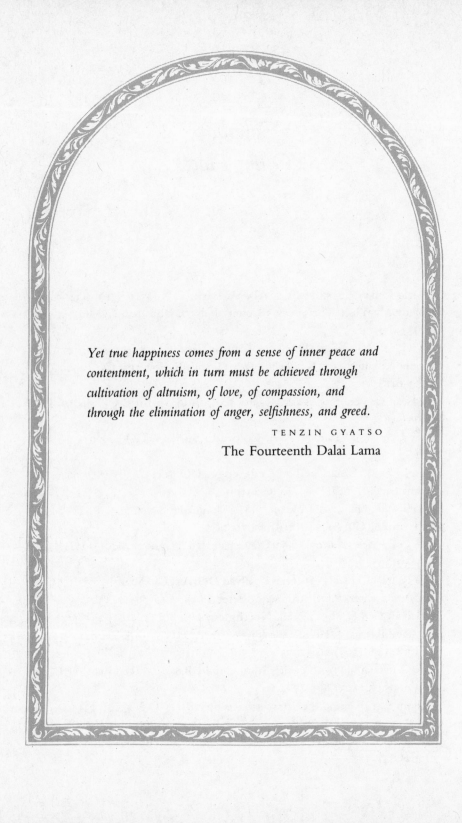

Yet true happiness comes from a sense of inner peace and contentment, which in turn must be achieved through cultivation of altruism, of love, of compassion, and through the elimination of anger, selfishness, and greed.

TENZIN GYATSO
The Fourteenth Dalai Lama

New Mexico

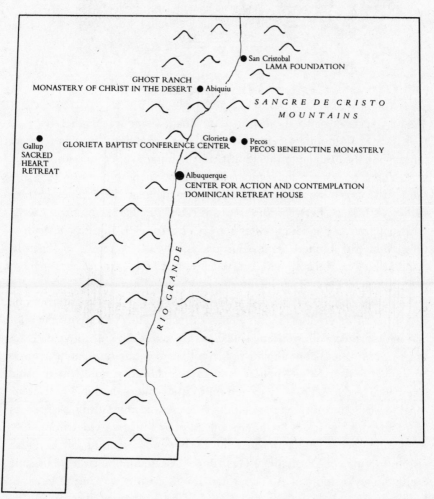

San Cristobal
LAMA FOUNDATION

GHOST RANCH
MONASTERY OF CHRIST IN THE DESERT ● Abiquiu

SANGRE DE CRISTO
MOUNTAINS

Gallup
SACRED
HEART
RETREAT

GLORIETA BAPTIST CONFERENCE CENTER

Glorieta ● Pecos
PECOS BENEDICTINE MONASTERY

Albuquerque
CENTER FOR ACTION AND CONTEMPLATION
DOMINICAN RETREAT HOUSE

RIO GRANDE

Center for Action and Contemplation
Albuquerque, NM

After 15 years of pastoral work in Cincinnati, Franciscan Father Richard Rohr came to Albuquerque in the mid-1980s to establish a formation center for laypeople to integrate their spirituality with active, compassionate service. Those who were doing inner work needed activity, he reasoned, and those who were serving others needed to deepen their experience of silence. A balance between the two was called for. Father Rohr is a well-known writer and a sought-after retreat director. His ministry takes him throughout the United States, Europe, and South America. His retreats examine the relationship between social justice and contemplative prayer, culminating in a social spirituality.

Since the center was founded, more than 40 people have spent from one to four months here learning the Franciscan way. They work with the poor and underprivileged, espousing social justice, wrestling with the paradoxes of being active and contemplative, Catholic and ecumenical, androgynous and enlightened, New Mexican and cross-cultural, playful, poetic, and humble all at once. Those who sign on to study, work, and live here come together daily for morning meditation. After prayer, the mornings are spent working with the poor, the afternoons in contemplative workshops.

In June 1990, CAC purchased the former mother house of the Franciscan Province of Our Lady of Guadalupe. Located in the largely Hispanic South Valley section of Albuquerque, this is within walking distance of Holy Family, a Franciscan parish church. The adobe structure called Tepayac House serves as a residence for long-term interns and short-term guests. There is a communal dining room, living room, and beds for about 15 in 11 rooms with shared baths. The community lives together like a large, bustling, caring family whose activities range far and wide. There is a sense of purposeful satisfaction as the daily chores of living flow smoothly from prayer to action to prayer again, like breathing out and in. "The biggest single benefit," Father Rohr points out, "is that this allows people to examine their own lives by helping others. . . . Mere liberalism and activism are not enough. . . . The challenge is to identify where you are *and* where you go from here."

Center for Action and Contemplation
P.O. Box 12464
1705 Five Points Rd. SW
Albuquerque, NM 87195
(505) 242-9588

Accommodations: *11 rooms for up to 15 men, women, and children, including interns, guests, and those temporarily without a home; residents share cooking for dinner together, and food is available for those who wish to prepare their own breakfast and lunch; 7:30 A.M. meditation at center Monday–Friday; mass monthly at center; 2:00–3:30 P.M. Scripture study or contemplative seminar once each week for participants in intern program and others; open year-round; $15–$25 a day based on ability to pay.*

Directions: *South on I-25 to approximately 3 miles south of junction with I-40, exit on Stadium Blvd. and turn right (west) for 3½ miles to Five Points Rd. Turn right on Five Points Rd. and go ¼ mile to guesthouse.*

Dominican Retreat House
Albuquerque, NM

A little over a mile outside Albuquerque, on 70 acres of desert floor, with views to the north and east of the Sandia and Monzano mountains, sit the unobtrusive buildings of a small community of nuns whose charm and hospitality are well known and long remembered by those who visit. The Dominican sisters, whose order opened the first retreat house for women in the United States in 1882, have staffed this center for more than 30 years. Following the dictum of St. Catherine de Ricci—"We have to see God's will and our work in the circumstance of the hour"—the sisters have evolved an annual schedule of weekend retreats to provide for the spiritual needs of as many people as possible. Their programs include silent prayer and fasting, Enneagram workshops, and 12-step support groups, as well as a number of directed retreats. During the week, there are days and evenings of reflection offered in both English and Spanish, serving the large Hispanic population of the Southwest.

The conference room—a converted hangar where the previous owner kept an airplane—is now an efficient meeting space. There are several lounges, a library, and a dining room. As many as 36 people can be accommodated in homelike private rooms with shared baths. There are four hermitage units in one building, each self-contained with private bath and kitchenette, air-conditioned or heated, stocked for retreatants to prepare their own breakfast and lunch. The evening meal can be taken with the community if desired. In addition to the main chapel, where guests can join the community for morning and evening prayer, there is a separate desert chapel, just a short distance from the main buildings. The adobe structure, with windows looking out over the surrounding desert, is a perfect place for meditation and contemplation.

Visitors feel as though they are stepping into a different world. As one retreatant said, "I get so much, I really don't know what it is, but I come back as often as I can."

Dominican Retreat House
5825 Coors Rd. SW
Albuquerque, NM 87121
(505) 877-4211

Accommodations: *36 beds in 31 rooms for men, women, and children, plus 4 hermitages; served meals in main dining room; mass daily in adobe chapel and morning and evening office; 70 acres in desert; closed August; $25 a day and $10 for spiritual direction; $55 for weekend program.*

Directions: *I-40 to Coors Rd. The retreat house is 2⁷⁄₁₀ miles south of Rio Bravo.*

ost Ranch

biquiu, NM

Ghost Ranch, with its towering mesas, is located on 21,000 acres of magnificent high desert, 6,500 feet above sea level. Donated to the Presbyterian church by the Pack family in 1955, it operates as a spiritually oriented conference center and antidote to the dangers inherent in a technologically oriented and mechanized society. Since the early 1970s, regular seminars have been offered to all those interested in paleontology, sociology, theology, education, history, literature, music, psychology, and environmental concerns.

This area was a swamp 250 million years ago, and after important fossil remains were found, the ranch was designated a Registered Natural Landmark because "the site possesses exceptional value as an illustration of the nation's heritage and contributes to a better understanding of man's environment."

The spectacular landscape attracted the artist Georgia O'Keeffe in the 1930s. She bought land nearby in 1940 and lived here until her death in 1986 painting the cliffs and sky, bones, trees, and mountains. Her well-known masterpieces embody the grandeur, simplicity, and amazing colors of this part of the Southwest.

There is a blend of cultures in the area—the Jicarilla–Apache and Navajo in nearby pueblos, the Hispanic community, and the recently arrived Anglo-Americans. Each group lives with shared concerns for the fragile ecology.

The ranch receives an annual average of only ten inches of rain, so the land is managed with exceptional care. Neighbors can use the pastureland to graze 400 to 600 cattle as conservation practices permit.

The guest facilities can accommodate up to 350 persons in plain but comfortable rooms with community washrooms. Meals are taken in a centrally located dining hall. During the summer season, due to the many programs offered, the rooms are often fully booked. During the rest of the year, there are conferences for smaller groups and monthlong courses in photography, pottery, and the like. Private retreatants are welcomed. There is an excellent library and chapel.

The real magic here is the setting for hiking and observation: seeing the early sun accentuate Chimney Rock, looking across the desert to the rock mesas outlined in the bluer-than-blue sky, and the stars at night in the clear New Mexican air.

Ghost Ranch
Abiquiu, NM 87510
(505) 685-4333

Accommodations: *Simple accommodations for 350 men, women, and children in singles, doubles, bunks, tepees, adobe casitas, 3 hogans, and 2 campgrounds accommodating 100 campers; cafeteria meals with vegetarian selections; swimming pools, hiking trails through stunning terrain, courses in Bible, ethics, theology, pottery, photography, riding, spiritual retreats, children's programs, anthropology, paleontology, solar housing program, local land use programs; unique geological formations and archeological areas of interest on property and nearby; 21,000 acres, 6,500-ft. altitude; open year-round; $36.75 a day in winter, $34.75 a day in summer, plus course price if taking one; special January term is $750 for the month all-inclusive, plus course materials for photography, geology, weaving, or watercolor classes.*

Directions: *Northwest of Santa Fe, NM, some 40 miles beyond Espanola on U.S. 84. Watch for the* GHOST RANCH *sign on the entrance gate between mileposts 224 and 225.*

Glorieta Baptist Conference Center
Glorieta, NM

Along the route of the old Santa Fe Trail, just 18 miles from the town of Santa Fe, is 2,500 acres of land owned by the Glorieta Baptist Conference Center. Surrounded by the 380,000-acre Santa Fe National Forest, much of which is preserved as wilderness, the center is in an enviable location for those seeking a mountain retreat.

In the late 1940s, foresightful Baptist leaders, looking for a meeting center in the West, dreamed of a place high in the mountains of New Mexico. The site, a former ranch, was bought privately on faith and held by mortgage until forces in the Baptist church were persuaded this was the right spot. And what these visionaries foresaw has become a reality. The complex has grown to a major facility of more than 150 buildings that can accommodate 2,700 guests. The facilities range from a deluxe hotel to camping spaces, lodge rooms with community baths to private apartments, cottages, and primitive cabins with nearby bathhouses. Every age and pocketbook can be satisfied, and all come to participate in the full range of programs that are available year-round. From Bible study, church music, and Sunday school leadership to missionary work and many children's programs, the schedule is all-inclusive. There are related activities for preschoolers and young children. In winter there are weeklong ski packages. At one of the first large gatherings here, held in 1952, the center was defined as a church leadership training center for every phase of Baptist life and work, a place of decision and life dedication.

At 7,500 feet in the Sangre de Cristo Mountains, there are numerous hiking trails from easy to rigorous, giving naturalists an easy opportunity to explore the rugged terrain. Or one can walk the seven miles of paved roads and admire the landscaping. Many of the annuals are grown in Glorieta's greenhouses, and up to 30,000 new flowers are planted each year.

The regular staff of more than 100 keeps the center functioning year-round. It is used by local churches, educational institutions, and other Christian and benevolent organizations that are attracted by the first-rate facilities, quiet setting, and the scenery.

Glorieta Baptist Conference Center
P.O. Box 8
Glorieta, NM 87535
(505) 757-6161

Accommodations: *Can accommodate 2,700 men, women, and children in summer and 1,500 in winter, in hotels/motels on property, apartments, rustic cottages, primitive cabins, RV and tent spaces; 3 meals a day in dining hall that can hold up to 1,500 people; 37,530 sq. ft. of conference space; 2,500 acres surrounded by 380,000-acre Santa Fe National Forest; gardens, tennis, badminton, miniature golf, marked hiking trails, events, courses, ski programs and packages, Chautauquas, Bible study, church leadership training; open year-round; from $66.70 a day including meals to $6 a day for certain campsites.*

Directions: *I-25 North from Santa Fe 18 miles to Glorieta (Exit 299). Turn left off ramp, left at* CONFERENCE CENTER *sign; ½ mile to entrance.*

Lama Foundation
San Cristobal, NM

The Lama Foundation is located 19 miles from Taos at 8,600 feet in the Sangre de Cristo Mountains. The complex of buildings sits on the side of Lama Mountain looking west across the broad expanse of the Rio Grande Gorge. In the late 1960s a group of Hippie activists came here to start a community following the teachings of the Indian guru Meher Baba. They were aided and encouraged by several American teachers such as Pir Vilayat Khan, Ram Dass, and Sam Lewis, who commingled their visions to establish a place that would serve to draw all religions together to celebrate the one truth . . . many paths but one mountain.

The 100 acres of pine woods, bordering the Kit Carson National Forest, is approached along a winding dirt road that slowly works its way up the mountain. Cars are parked below the buildings and living quarters and camping areas are reached on foot. A community of about 20 hardy people live here year-round and take their meals together in the centrally positioned dining room—a rustic, charming wooden building that also serves as a meeting place. The bells on the rack outside were made from the nose cones of ballistic missiles. Just a short distance away sits the main temple or meditation hall, with its 44-foot geodesic dome, where large groups gather. There is a library in one section and a smaller cavelike meditation chamber where groups of 10 to 12 can share the synergy of their spiritual force.

There are A-frames and small domed buildings throughout the woods and an adobe structure with kitchen, dining room, prayer room, and 12 rooms for guests built around a central courtyard. Buildings are lighted by kerosene lamps and heated by woodburning stoves, and there are outdoor privies. Community members must attend a community meditation session daily in addition to performing another practice of their own choice such as yoga or t'ai chi ch'uan. Each person has a daily work commitment such as cleaning, cooking, or wood gathering. There are cottage industries that make and sell colorful prayer flags, banners, and T-shirts, and there is also a book service. The summer season sees the community double in size to put on the summer programs, which begin about mid-May and continue through September. The topics of the weekend and weeklong sessions deal with spiritual development and awakening, music, ecology, and dance.

In the mid-1980s, Father Thomas Keating held a retreat here with a group that evolved into the Chrysalis Movement, a network of Catholic lay communities that focus on community service, centering prayer, and contemplative living. In 1970, Ram Dass collaborated with the Lama community to produce his famous book, *Be Here Now*. Up the mountain, above the dwellings, is the final resting place of Samuel Lewis, affectionately remembered as "Sufi Sam."

The community is evolving and is a way station where pilgrims find shelter from outer-world distraction and a greenhouse where early spiritual awakening is protected and nurtured . . . it is a blending of East and West and a place of hope for peace on earth.

Lama Foundation
P.O. Box 240
San Cristobal, NM 87564
(505) 586-1269 (10 A.M. to noon mountain time)

Accommodations: For men, women, and children, 12 private rooms, 2 retreat hermitages, 2 dorms, tents, and tepees. Sometimes 150 people stay on the land for summer programs; solar showers; nice outhouses, delicious home-grown, organic, vegetarian food served on picnic tables in summer; daily meditation; courses, classes, yoga, practices of all spiritual paths; spring workcamp—live, work, practice, and play for $10 a day to set up for summer (and a good way to learn about life at Lama); pool, pond, good child-care program; open to public for summer programs, for community only in winter; $18 a day for hermitages, $5 a day in dorm; bring own tents for camping; $240 a month for summer staff until you reach $1,500, then no fee; course fees include room and board.

Directions: 19 miles north of Taos on Rte. 522 look for the small green LAMA sign just before the turnoff. Turn east at the trailer/lumberyard, drive over the cattle guard, and follow the signs to Lama, about 4 miles uphill. Drive slowly.

Monastery of Christ in the Desert
Abiquiu, NM

The stories of the difficulties encountered reaching this spiritual outpost are legion. Many have driven partway, become mired in the mud, and had to walk in. The 12-mile dirt road is treacherous at best and even the grazing cattle disdain it. But once there, deep in Chaco Canyon, with the Chaco River flowing nearby, one can feel the difference in the air . . . "saturated in peace," as one visitor noted, "like bread soaked in wine. The obvious stillness, so striking in contrast to most other places, has a lot to do with the spectacular location . . . remote and beautiful by any standard."

Founded by Father Aelred Well, a Benedictine priest who came here with two other monks in 1964 from Mount Saviour Monastery in Pine City, NY (see *Sanctuaries—The Northeast,* pp. 148–49), they enlisted George Nakashima, the famous Japanese-American woodworker, as architect. His genius with wood and his approach to the functional use of structure that blends with surroundings is one of the highest forms of artistic achievement.

Hundreds of people come here each year to spend a day or more, joining the dozen or so monks in the routine of their monastic life. Guests join the community for common prayer in the chapel, where the windows look out on the red cliffs of the mesa and the whole canyon appears to be a chapel. "I feel this is a way stop to heaven," said one visitor.

Meals are taken with the monks in the refectory. The midday meal is accompanied by taped classical music; at the evening meal one of the monks reads psalms or a book of general interest. The food is vegetarian, well-prepared, nourishing, and delicious.

There are no formal retreats, but guests can arrange ahead to speak with one of the monks. Those who come are encouraged to seek Christ in the desert in their own way. The monks offer hospitality and the sharing of their Benedictine way of life. The key elements are love for one another, prayer, reading, study, and manual labor. Visitors are expected to work at least some of the time, as this is one of the elements of a balanced monastic day. There are stations of the cross that zigzag up the side of one of the mesas. The 12th station, the Crucifixion, looks over the entire monastery.

An extra amount of preparation is necessary for a visit here, such as proper clothing, since the snowy winters are very cold. Guest rooms are heated with woodstoves and lighted by kerosene lamps. Summer days are warm, then cool in the mornings. Shorts are not permitted in chapel, refectory, or guest house areas. A flashlight is useful, as are sturdy walking or hiking shoes. Musical instruments, tape recorders, or radios should not be played as sound carries and one is expected to be sensitive to others. There is no telephone—the nearest is 15 miles away at Ghost Ranch—but one can glory in giving up the trappings of civilization for just a little while to encounter Christ, who waits for us in the desert.

Monastery of Christ in the Desert
Abiquiu, NM 87510

Accommodations: 17 beds for men and women in singles and doubles, with woodburning stoves and kerosene lamps; there is hot and cold running water in the bathrooms; nonmeat meals in silence in refectory with music or table reading; daily Eucharist and prayer services with Gregorian chant; located in an isolated and beautiful desert canyon 6,500 feet above sea level, adjoining the National Wilderness for hiking; nearest telephone 15 miles away; open year-round; no fixed charge—$20 a night covers expenses but each guest must decide what she or he can afford.

Directions: 75 miles north of Santa Fe, NM, and 53 miles south of Chama, NM, off U.S. Rte. 84. About 1 mile south of the entrance sign for Echo Amphi-theater, or 1 mile north of the Ghost Ranch Visitors' Center of the Carson National Forest (not to be confused with Ghost Ranch itself), the road for the monastery leaves Rte. 84 toward the west (from Santa Fe turn left) onto Forest Service Rd. 151. It is a winding, steep, and narrow road, with a dirt and clay surface that becomes very slippery when wet. Drivers should allow time for the road to dry after a rain; in winter it's safest when frozen (during the night and early morning before sunrise). Don't take chances—this 12-mile road has been walked by many stranded drivers.

Pecos Benedictine Monastery
Pecos, NM

The adobe buildings of this monastery located in the Pecos River valley blend perfectly with the surrounding Sangre de Cristo Mountains. This 900-acre property was acquired by Catholic Benedictine monks who came here in 1955 seeking a place where solitude and space were readily available. From its very beginnings, the monastery has served as a center for retreats and church renewal. The first cursillo in the United States was held here, and the community has been consistently involved with marriage encounter and family retreats.

One of the distinguishing marks of this monastery, perhaps a precursor in monastic evolution, is that in 1969 the community welcomed four monks from Benet Lake, WI, who shared a vision of establishing a Charismatic Benedictine way of life. This has become a reality here and the monastery enjoys a wide reputation for Charismatic renewal. Twice a year there are monthlong training sessions called School for Charismatic Spiritual Directors, where individuals are trained to serve their home communities. Directed and private retreats are welcome. The community gathers four times a day for prayer in the chapel, and there is daily mass. The rooms are snug and comfortable. Corridors connect the guest quarters with the dining room and chapel. This is a bonus in the winter, when heavy snow accumulates.

Another distinguishing mark of Pecos is that monastic men and women live together following five promises: obedience, conversion of life, stability, poverty, and chastity. Men and women living together as one community has long been sanctioned by the Church. As this communal call unfolded, Pecos realized the need to join a congregation that would nurture this vision. So in 1985, after a three-year trial period, Pecos officially became part of the Olivetan Congregation of Sienna, Italy. This group, founded by Blessed Bernard Tolamel in 1319, has from its beginning been composed of men and women.

The Pecos community believes the golden thread that holds it together is stated by St. Benedict's Rule: "Let all guests to the monastery be received as Christ Himself." The community concentrates on mystical experiences, cultivating an experiential approach rather than teaching. As one monk stated, "Religion is caught, not taught. In ten years the Catholic church will be very different, more experiential and less based on the service station approach, more responsive and participatory. We can't afford to be myopic . . . lay ministry has to be drawn in."

Pecos Benedictine Monastery
Pecos NM 87552
(505) 757-6415

Accommodations: *Double and triple rooms with private baths for 65 men and women; healthful family-style meals at tables of 8 with community; daily mass plus prayer 4 times daily; Charismatic healing and other renewal retreats and school for spiritual directors; 900 acres in Pecos River valley surrounded by 13,000-ft. mountains; hiking trails; open year-round; suggested donation: $35 a day.*

Directions: *Rte. 25 North from Santa Fe 18 miles to Glorieta (Exit 299); follow sign to Pecos 7 miles and take Rte. 63 North to the monastery.*

Sacred Heart Retreat
Gallup, NM

Perched on a hilltop, looking across a desert valley to the town of Gallup, and surrounded by Navajo reservation lands, sit the 16 acres of the Sacred Heart Retreat. In the parking lot, shared with the local parish, there is a well from which the Indians draw water at all hours of the day. Many of the retreat's guest buildings are Indian hogans: six-sided buildings of logs laid one on the other and sealed. There is a single door and a skylight in the center of the roof from which, in the past, the smoke of heating and cooking fires could escape; but these hogans are now heated electrically, have shared bathrooms, and are comfortably furnished so that camping here is no strain at all. The facilities will accommodate 58 people, and the programs and retreats held here are very popular. Most weekends are booked six months ahead.

There is a small community of Catholic sisters, Auxiliaries of the Blessed Sacrament, who live here and work with the lay retreat director and the nearby parish priest to make the center an attractive and hospitable place. There is daily mass in the chapel at 7 A.M.; the sisters meet for prayer and meditation prior to mass and guests are welcome to join them. The chapel, built on a crest, has commanding views to the north and west, and the lights of the town twinkle at night in the clear desert air.

There is an inviting wood-paneled dining room with a stone fireplace and large windows. Hearty meals are prepared by the sisters. Coffee and tea are regularly available.

Built as a diocesan retreat center in the early 1970s by Bishop Jerome Hastrich, the facilities have grown in scope and have become the meeting place for weekend deaconite programs, one specifically for Native Americans. The programs encompass diocesan councils and conferences for educators, many youth meetings, and vocation retreats for men and women, as well as special courses for groups such as the National Evangelical Team (NET) for teenagers and the United Methodist Women. Private retreatants are accommodated and encouraged. Spiritual direction can be arranged from a local priest or deacon.

Sacred Heart Retreat
P.O. Box 1989
Gallup, NM 87301
(505) 722-6755

Accommodations: *Comfortable singles and doubles for 58 men, women, and children in main building and 5 Indian hogans (8-sided buildings); home-cooked buffet in well-designed dining room looking out to valley at round tables for 5; morning, afternoon, and evening prayer, plus mass daily; 16 acres of hilltop with trails and benches; surrounded by Navajo reservation; open year-round; $25 a day suggested donation according to your means and length of stay.*

Directions: *2 miles south of Gallup on Zuni Rd. Take 1-40 to 602 Bypass. Just past Nizhoni Blvd. is a set of stoplights. Continue on 602 1⁷⁄₁₀ miles (past De Ann St.) to a left turn uphill to Sacred Heart Retreat and St. Jerome's Parish.*

New Mexico:
Other Places

Tres Rios Christian Center, 1159 Black River Village Rd., **Carlsbad,** NM 88220. (505) 785-2361

Bodhi Mandala, P.O. Box 8, **Jemez Springs,** NM 87025. (505) 829-3854

Rose Mountain Retreat Center, P.O. Box 355, **Las Vegas,** NM 87701. (505) 425-5728

Holy Cross Retreat Center, P.O. Box 158, **Mesilla Park,** NM 88047. (505) 524-3688

Ocamora Foundation, P.O. Box 43, **Ocate,** NM 87734. (505) 666-2389

Takoja Retreats, 656 N. Star Rte., **Questa,** NM 87556. (505) 586-1086

Immaculate Heart of Mary Conference Center, Mt. Carmel Rd., **Santa Fe,** NM 87501. (505) 983-3494

Mountain Cloud Zen Center, Rte. 7, 125 MC Old Santa Fe Trail, **Santa Fe,** NM 87505. (505) 988-4396

Sangre de Cristo Center, Rte. 4, **Santa Fe,** NM 87501. (505) 983-7291

Mable Dodge Luhan B&B, P.O. Box 1529, **Taos,** NM 87571. (505) 758-9456

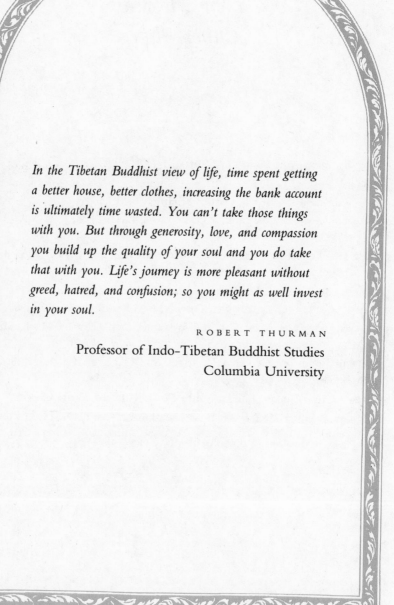

*In the Tibetan Buddhist view of life, time spent getting
a better house, better clothes, increasing the bank account
is ultimately time wasted. You can't take those things
with you. But through generosity, love, and compassion
you build up the quality of your soul and you do take
that with you. Life's journey is more pleasant without
greed, hatred, and confusion; so you might as well invest
in your soul.*

ROBERT THURMAN
Professor of Indo-Tibetan Buddhist Studies
Columbia University

O*regon*

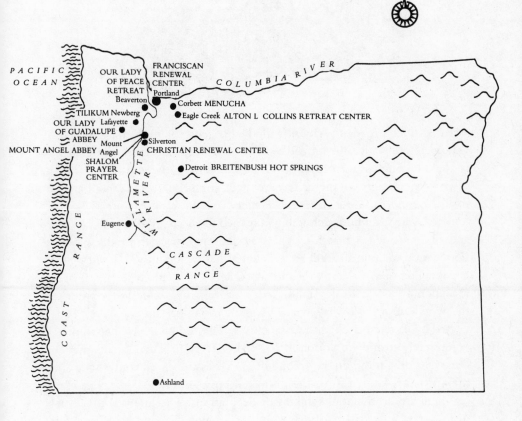

PACIFIC
OCEAN

OUR LADY
OF PEACE
RETREAT
Beaverton

FRANCISCAN
RENEWAL
CENTER
Portland

COLUMBIA RIVER

Corbett MENUCHA

TILIKUM Newberg
OUR LADY
OF GUADALUPE
ABBEY
MOUNT ANGEL ABBEY

Lafayette

Mount
Angel

Eagle Creek ALTON L COLLINS RETREAT CENTER

Silverton
CHRISTIAN RENEWAL CENTER

SHALOM
PRAYER
CENTER

Detroit BREITENBUSH HOT SPRINGS

WILLAMETTE RIVER

Eugene

CASCADE

RANGE

COAST RANGE

Ashland

Alton L. Collins Retreat Center
Eagle Creek, OR

Off one of the roads to Mount Hood, this center is tucked away in the Cascade woodlands. Surrounded by tall cedars and Douglas firs, the shingle-roofed building has the proportions of a cathedral but was so well planned it seems to have grown there. The architect, John Kyle, won a merit award for the design from the American Society of Landscape Architects.

The United Methodist church had owned the 68 acres of land since 1940 and was awarded a matching grant in the late 1970s from the Collins Foundation to build an adult retreat center that would provide a setting for encouraging spiritual growth and awareness. The structure has a large reception area next to the dining room and picture windows look out to the woods across a lower lawn. The guest rooms are on two levels connected by covered decks and passageways. The rooms are well appointed, comfortably furnished, and each has a private bath. There is an inviting library-reading room on the second floor. Meals are served family-style and the kitchen is known for its home-baked bread and rolls.

There are no religious symbols or decorations. The intent is to accentuate a renewal with nature by understatement. Groups have found it especially beneficial to meet here, be able to focus, and get things done. Elderhostel programs take place up to 20 weeks each year, aiming for in-depth examination and exploration of social issues, music study, and history. Private retreatants can be accommodated on a space-available basis.

There are hiking trails through the mature-growth woods, which are unspoiled, almost primeval—"just the way God meant them to be," a spokesman pointed out. The property is bordered by Deep Creek, which flows into the Clackamas River.

Alton L. Collins Retreat Center
32867 SE Hwy. 211
Eagle Creek, OR 97022
(503) 637-6411

Accommodations: *Lovely double rooms looking out to woods, for men and women (some with capacity for 4 people) to accommodate a total of 40–66; home-cooked meals for groups; if no groups on site, then private retreatants must dine nearby (refrigerator, but no stove accessible); can serve 120 in dining room looking out to landscaped garden and magnificent western red cedars; organic garden produces 4,000 pounds of vegetables each summer; 68 acres with hiking trails, volleyball, Ping-Pong; located in Cascade woodlands with Mt. Hood, Clackamas River, Columbia River gorge nearby; open year-round; $42 a day.*

Directions: *30 miles southeast of Portland. From the south take I-5 to I-205 and exit at Hwy. 224 (Mt. Hood exit). Follow Hwy. 224 to Eagle Creek (14 miles from freeway) and turn left on Hwy. 211 for 2 miles to the center drive on the left.*

Breitenbush Hot Springs
Detroit, OR

Named after Peter Breitenbush, who explored the Willamette Valley in the 1840s, these hot springs were used by Native Americans for centuries. The different tribes set aside their rivalries and feuds during their time here, recognizing this to be a sacred place for healing. Located in the Cascade Mountains, the springs are surrounded by the Willamette National Forest with its mountains, canyons, cascading streams, and rivers. The Breitenbush River flows through the 86 acres of the retreat, and these rushing waters, through the use of an ingenious hydroelectric plant, provide the electricity for the center; geothermal heat is taken from the same source that provides the artesian-flow hot springs.

A group of 35 people lives on the grounds, maintains the more than 40 rustic cabins, provides three well-prepared vegetarian meals a day, and organizes an array of programs and services that satisfy the most eclectic tastes. The community is committed to sharing its spiritual practice with all guests. There is daily morning meditation, a yoga session, and a spiritual maintenance program called EDGU—a series of upper-body movements that is excellent for rehabilitating the back.

The scheduled events, usually around weekends, offer courses in relationships, including men's and women's issues, healing arts, massage and bodywork, the environment, and self-transformation such as holotropic breathwork and fire walking. Evening activities include concerts, storytelling, drumming circles, singalongs, and dancing. There is a monthly sweat lodge ceremony. Elderhostel courses are given in forest ecology.

There is a parking area at the edge of the property where you
bags into a cart in order to reach the snug, wooden cabins, all of wh
heat and electricity and basic furnishings but only about half of which nave
plumbing. There are community bathhouses nearby. Bedding can be rented
or you can bring your own sleeping bag.

The staff offers full-body or focused-area massage, as well as hydrother-
apy and herbal wrap. The several hot springs are a delight to slip into on a
cold night, with only the sounds of the river flowing nearby, the outline of
the mountains delineated against the clear, star-marked sky.

"Breitenbush," as founder Alex Beamer wrote, "is a grand experiment
to find better ways for people to live, work, and play together. We explore
and practice helping others evolve to their highest potential, through psychological processing, spiritual practice, having fun, serving others, and
taking good care of the body. We honor all paths respectful of people and
the earth."

Breitenbush Hot Springs
P.O. Box 578
Detroit, OR 97342
(503) 854-3314

Accommodations: *More than 40 rustic cabins with electricity and heat for men,
women, and children, some with private baths, some with 2 bedrooms, all with
double bed plus 1–2 other beds or bunks and platform tents with mattresses; tasty
home-cooked vegetarian meals; daily meditation, morning circle (in Sanctuary),
EDGU, yoga; property surrounded by 1⁹⁄₁₀-million-acre Willamette National Forest; weekend programs from ancient forest hikes to expanding your inner light;
cross-country skiing, journal-writing workshops, fire walking instructors' training;
massage available; swimming hole, 4 geothermal hot tubs with bathing suits optional, meadow pools with natural hot springs overlooking river, mountains; hot
natural steam sauna with cold water tub; evening storytelling in front of fire, jam
sessions, etc.; open year-round; $50 a day per person with 2 in a room, $60–$70 per
person in private cabin, includes 3 meals; bedding and towel rental available if you
don't bring your own.*

Directions: *I-5 North to Hwy. 22 East to Detroit, OR. At only gas station in
town turn left onto Hwy. 46 (see BREITENBUSH 10 MILES sign). 100 feet past Cleator
Bend Campground take a right over bridge and follow signs, taking every left turn
after bridge to Breitenbush parking lot.*

Christian Renewal Center
Silverton, OR

In 1971, Lutheran minister Allan Hansen and wife, Eunice, dreamed of establishing a remote retreat where Christian families could come for a rest and children would have a place of happy memories connected to their faith. Having lived in Southern California for 25 years, the only stipulation they had was that the place should be in the hills or mountains and have a plenteous supply of trees and water. They had a legacy of $7,000 in a fund they called the Lord's Money. One day a relative called from Oregon to say: "I've found some land for sale but I don't think you'll like it." "Why not?" Hansen asked. "Well, it's very remote, in the mountains next to a state park, covered with trees . . . and the seller wants the money tomorrow." "How much?" Hansen asked. "$7,000," came the reply. The Hansens wired the money that day and bought the 40 acres sight unseen.

Since then, they have erected 16 buildings of varying sizes and shapes on the side of the hill and developed a family-oriented retreat center with a staff of 20. Over the years, people came to visit, liked what they saw, and signed on to stay. The community meets daily around noon for a prayer service. Its mission is to provide spiritually oriented groups, families, and individuals with a quiet, peaceful place for rest and renewal.

There is a variety of accommodations in the lodges and chalets. The buildings are snug, comfortably furnished, and decorated with charm. Visitors should bring their own sleeping bags or bedding, pillows, and towels. There are community bathrooms and showers. The larger lodges have meeting areas inside. The chapel seats 50 for services or a gathering. Each building is in its own woodland setting, and trails lead from one to the other. At one place there is a cable strung between two trees over a slope in the land and a sling chair takes the adventurous from one side to the other—a great experience for child or adult.

Each summer, the center invites well-known Evangelical ministers to spend a week presenting programs of spiritual awakening, prayer, and healing through faith. In 1991, the ministers were Presbyterian, Lutheran, Catholic, Mennonite, and Evangelical sisters, representing the ecumenical attitude of the center. Private retreatants and families are welcome throughout the year.

The property is at the edge of Silver Falls State Park, which has many hiking trails. One leads past ten magnificent waterfalls, the highest from 184 feet, another over 170 feet. The view from the deck off the main dining room looks down a draw to the rolling, forested mountains.

Christian Renewal Center
22444 N. Fork Rd. SE
Silverton, OR 97381
(503) 873-6743

Accommodations: *For Christian families of all denominations, accommodations for up to 125 in a variety of charming cabins and lodges on this 40-acre property; good home-cooked meals—bread, soup, cakes, hot cereals, homemade granola, soufflés, french toast—in lovely lodge dining room overlooking fir-covered hills and valleys; the summer program consists of singing, lectures, quiet time, and prayer groups in the morning; afternoons provide recreation—crafts, hikes, picnics, volleyball, horseshoes, Ping-Pong, swinging bridge, cable ride, treehouse; property adjoins Silver Falls State Park with 10 spectacular waterfalls; open year-round; summer program on a donation basis; other times of the year church groups rent the facilities at $25–$30 a day per person; space for private retreatants available weekdays except in summer.*

Directions: *30 miles east of Salem. Take Rte. 22 East from Salem, then Rte. 214 for 30 miles all the way through Silver Falls State Park. Turn left on N. Fork Rd. opposite the N. Falls parking lot.*

Franciscan Renewal Center
Portland, OR

Across the road from Lewis and Clark College, at the top of Palatine Hill, the Franciscan Renewal Center sits serene and quiet on 20 acres. The landscaped grounds are surrounded by cedar and fir trees, giving a sense of privacy and seclusion. The property was purchased in 1942 by the Sisters of St. Francis for novitiate training and subsequently became the headquarters of the Western Province Franciscans. During the 1950s, many buildings were added to house and school novices. The beautiful Our Lady of Angels chapel was dedicated in 1958. In 1981, the mission of the school facilities was redirected for retreats and conferences.

The centerpoint of the complex is the former Corbett mansion, which was built in the late 1920s. Designed by Pietro Belluschi, it has a combination of architectural styles: the arrangement and proportioning of the windows suggest a European château; the extensive use of weathered brick from a razed brewery looks Georgian. The 40-room mansion is impressive and grand, and adds character to the complex.

The retreat wing is a separate building on three levels. The upper two floors have rooms for 60—26 singles and 17 doubles—with community men's and women's bathrooms. The lower level has conference rooms, a kitchen for snacks and hot drinks, and an elegant library-reading room. The dining room is in a nearby building, where meals are served cafeteria-style. The sisters who live here often have guests join them at meals; larger groups use an adjacent dining room.

There is a series of spiritual programs and retreats from one-day meetings to weekends, and a six-day silent retreat. There are a number of Elderhostel programs as well as classes to learn Spanish and an ongoing series on centering prayer following the teachings of Father Thomas Keating. Private, directed, and guided retreats are available throughout the year.

There is a quiet, restful ambience here nurtured by the welcoming sisters. The grounds are a pleasure to stroll.

Franciscan Renewal Center
0858 SW Palatine Hill Rd.
Portland, OR 97219
(503) 636-1590

Accommodations: *26 singles and 17 doubles for 60 men and women; community baths with nice touches like hand lotion and terry hand towels; home-cooked meals, breads, pastries in a light, pleasant dining room looking out to grounds of convent; mass Monday–Friday in convent; 20 acres in hills of southwest Portland adjacent to Lewis and Clark College; landscaped grounds with orchards; closed 1 week in August and Christmas holidays; $31 a day.*

Directions: *From I-5 take Terwilliger exit (Exit 297). Follow* TERWILLIGER BLVD. *and* LEWIS AND CLARK COLLEGE *signs. Continue past Lewis and Clark campus (street is now called Palatine Hill Rd.). Turn right at first driveway with sign for center.*

Menucha Retreat and Conference Center
Corbett, OR

One of the approaches to Menucha from Portland, only 22 miles to the west, is along the old scenic highway that follows the contour of the Columbia River past waterfalls that tumble from heights of more than 100 feet. This 99-acre retreat is on a bluff 800 feet above the river where the views east and west of the great gorge are awesome. The site was purchased in 1950 by Portland's First Presbyterian Church as a place where individuals and groups could get away for a while to study, reflect, and renew. The Hebrew word *menucha* means rest, peace, or repose—an apt description for this inspirational location. One can't help but be calmed and quieted by the vast panoramas.

This was once the private home of Julius L. Meier, governor of Oregon from 1930 to 1934, and Presidents Herbert Hoover and Franklin Delano Roosevelt were guests here. The building, now called Wright Hall, was completed in 1927 and now contains the central dining room as well as a meeting area. The great hall, with its huge stone fireplace, is large enough to hold 100 people. There are also eight dormitory rooms with adjoining bathrooms for up to 48 persons in this pleasant building. Other facilities on the property offer homelike accommodations from an apartment for individuals or families to dormitory sleeping arrangements. There is an array of group meeting spaces for 10 to 50 in eight different buildings.

The professional staff that manages the facility seems unflappable while maintaining a country home atmosphere and making it possible for many to come and share the place. The spirituality of the setting seems to touch all who visit. As one guest noted, "This is the most nurturing center I've ever been in, and I've been in a bunch of 'em!"

There are trails through the woods and different viewpoints for looking across the gorge to the far mountains. Here tensions can be reduced and the mind becomes still. On the wall of the manager's office hangs a reminder: "What I do today is very important, because I am exchanging a day of my life for it."

Menucha Retreat and Conference Center
38711 E. Crown Point Hwy.
P. O. Box 8
Corbett, OR 97019
(503) 695-2243

Accommodations: *160 beds for men, women, and children in semiprivate rooms, and dorms, in 8 separate sleeping areas; delicious home-cooked meals with homemade bread and cookies; 99 acres on bluff overlooking the Columbia River gorge with hiking, swimming, tennis; open year-round except for a few days at Christmas; $33 a day, with special rates for longer stays or private room or cottage.*

Directions: *22 miles east of Portland via I-84 to Corbett, Exit 22. Drive up Corbett Hill Rd. to the Scenic Hwy. Turn left and drive 1¼ miles east to the gate on the left.*

Mount Angel Abbey Retreat House
St. Benedict, OR

In the Willamette Valley, where lush farmland lies between the Cascade Mountains and the coast ranges, there has been a community of Benedictine monks for more than 100 years. In 1882, a contingent from Engelberg, Switzerland, came to the little town of Fillmore—the name was later changed to Mount Angel—and acquired over a thousand acres of land. The buildings of the abbey were eventually constructed on a butte overlooking the valley to meet the needs of the growing community whose history as a place of education is an integral part of the Northwest. Twice major fires destroyed part of the complex, but now the hilltop resembles a college campus where the main church is the focal point. Here the 55 monks come together six times a day to sing the canonical hours. The impressive church has a high vaulted roof over the altar and a choir section where the monks' double-row pews face each other, one side responding to the other during the sung liturgy. There is seating for hundreds in the main section, and Sunday services are very popular.

In 1970, the library building was completed. This 44,000-square-foot three-story structure was designed by the Finnish architect Alvar Aalto. Made possible by a donation from the Vollum family, the founder of Tektronix, the library houses more than 250,000 volumes in theology, language, philosophy, the arts, social sciences, and natural history. Designed to be user-friendly, the collection is on a state-of-the-art computer system and there are 70 nooks for individual study. There is a comfortable reading room with 600 current periodicals, a music listening room, and an auditorium that is an acoustically perfect space. There are more than 100 seminary students who live at the abbey and are engaged in undergraduate and graduate studies.

A few steps from the church, there is a retreat and guesthouse with 30 rooms, each with private bath. The rooms are nicely furnished and well maintained. A lower lounge has a snack area where hot drinks are always available. Meals are provided either here or in the seminary dining room in a building across the lawn. There is a separate chapel for quiet meditation and prayer.

The retreat programs are designed for contemporary spiritual needs reaching out to mothers and daughters, fathers and sons, married couples, as well as professional groups such as flight attendants, and groups from other religious denominations. Private retreatants are accommodated.

Years ago, stone seats were found on top of the hill where the buildings now stand. Local Indians revealed that their ancestors had used these stones when they wanted to speak with the Great Spirit. In those days the butte was called Tap-a-Lam-a-Ho, the Mount of Communion. "You call it Mount Angel," one Indian said, "and you built a more elaborate structure than the stone seats of the natives, but its purpose will forever be the same—a mount of communion and prayer for unknown ages."

Mount Angel Abbey Retreat House
St. Benedict, OR 97373
(503) 845-3025

Accommodations: *30 private rooms with twin beds, bath, and telephone in each for men, women, and children; cafeteria meals; mass plus prayer 6 times daily in substantial church; self-guided walking tour map; "Glad for What He Has Made," a lovely guide to the trees, shrubs, flowers and birds of Mount Angel Abbey; special retreat weekends including annual Bach Festival, artists' retreat, flight attendants' retreat; Easter retreat including a Passover dinner and wonderful Easter celebrations; outsiders can attend courses at the theological graduate school; beautiful library; closed 4th of July, Labor Day, Thanksgiving; suggested donation: $35 a day per person. The retreat house is often booked to capacity.*

Directions: *I-5 to Salem, Market St./Silverton exit from south. Follow signs to Mount Angel (Market to Lancaster to Silverton). Abbey is on right on far edge of town of Mount Angel on Rte. 213. From the north take Woodburn/Silverton exit and follow Rte. 214 to abbey on left.*

Our Lady of Guadalupe
Trappist Abbey

Lafayette, OR

In 1955, after seven years in New Mexico, this community moved to the farm country of Oregon seeking greater seclusion. Their property is 900 acres of woods and 400 acres of farmland. The long driveway winds through the fields to the monastery complex, which sits alone on the hilltop. The church overlooks a large courtyard, the guest refectory, and the bookstore. A passageway from the refectory leads to the four guest cottages. These duplex units share a bath at midlevel, are beautifully designed and connected by wooden decks, and look out over ponds and woods. The rooms are very comfortable and private with single bed, desk, reading lamp, and rocking chair. Meals are served in the refectory, where the monks set the tables and clear away afterward, kindly discouraging would-be helpers. The food is hearty, vegetarian, and delicious (especially the home-baked bread). Dinner, when we visited, was cooked by a doctor who had joined the community as part of their sabbatical residency program. Coffee and tea are always available in the dining area.

The 40 monks in the community—16 priests and 24 brothers—meet in the chapel to sing the canonical hours five times a day, with mass following 6:30 A.M. Lauds. On Sunday, mass is at 10:45 A.M. following Sext. The excellent acoustics of the wooden interior of the church accentuate the organ or guitar accompaniment; three monks can play the organ; three others are guitarists. The liturgy is beautifully arranged and sung.

Visitors are expected to structure their own time, but monks are available for discussion by appointment. There is a small library and tape selection in a pleasant reading room. Thomas Merton once wrote: "There is an advantage to the monastery by inviting people in and being in touch." The guestmaster paraphrased that statement by saying, "Guests have been an enrichment to us."

Retreatants can come for one to seven days. "It really takes two days to wind down," one monk noted, "stress being one of the main addictions of our society. Visitors should leave their books at home; whatever they need for security, leave it behind. Try to let it go and accept that it's OK without anything to do. *Don't just do something, sit there!* Many who come have reached a point in life where they have to change. Once they admit that, they'll be able to accept the process, let the transformation happen. As people work prayer into their schedule, then everything is prayer, all the time."

The main business of the monastery is bookbinding. About 20 of the monks produce as many as 1,000 volumes a week. More than 1,000 Douglas fir trees are planted on the property every year to replace the aging trees and the community tends an extensive vegetable garden.

The grounds are exceptionally peaceful to wander through. Trails lead past a large cottonwood tree, to ponds, and from the top of one of the hills the frosty peak of Mount Hood is visible. At night, frogs, coyotes, and hoot owls can be heard chanting their own litany.

Our Lady of Guadalupe Trappist Abbey
P.O. Box 97
Lafayette, OR 97127
(503) 852-0107

Accommodations: *Lovely duplex hermitages for men and women (4 units with 2 rooms each) looking out on pond or grounds; beautifully designed for space, tranquillity, ease of reading, prayer, comfort (each has heat and some a woodstove); buffet meals in retreatant dining room, homemade bread, large garden; prayer 5 times daily with lovely singing; 900 acres of hills, woods, hiking trails; library; new facility on hillside for group meditation, another room overlooking pond for added quiet space; work can be arranged; residency program where men can live with community for 2 months; open year-round; freewill donations ("Leave whatever your means allow— your generosity will be shared with those less fortunate"); reserve far in advance.*

Directions: *From Portland drive south on I-5 to the Tigard/Hwy. 99W exit. Turn right and stay on Hwy. 99W for 26 miles to Lafayette. At the west end of town, turn right onto Bridge St. and go north 3 miles on the surfaced road to the abbey on the right.*

Our Lady of Peace Retreat
Beaverton, OR

In a quiet suburb of Portland, the Franciscan Missionary Sisters of Our Lady of Sorrows were given 25 acres by Archbishop Howard in the 1950s on which to build a retreat house. Founded in China in the 1930s, this order was forced out by the Communists after World War II, and established a retreat center in Soquel, CA (see page 78). The Oregon property is their second foundation in the United States.

The single-story brick complex, surrounded by well-kept lawns dotted with fruit trees, has become an integral part of the urban neighborhood. The sisters, who wear black habits, have evolved a program of retreats that reach out to every conceivable possibility: weekends for only men or women, parent-teens, married couples, mothers with babies and/or toddlers, and one for the handicapped. For 19 years, they have held a two-week summer catechetical program to help individuals increase the knowledge of their faith and discern the will of God in today's world. There are many single-day retreats throughout the year, as well as a vocation-discernment day for those considering religious life. Private retreatants can be accommodated.

There are 60 rooms available, mostly single, with shared baths, and furnished with bed, table, and chair. Meals are taken cafeteria-style in the dining room, and the food is delicious. Freshly baked cookies are often available.

There are two chapels, one in the visitor's wing, where services are held during retreats. The sisters come together in their own chapel, where guests are welcome, for daily mass at 6:40 A.M., afternoon prayer around 4, then Compline after the evening meal.

There is an annual barbecue and festival, when more than 1,000 people come to enjoy the food and live music and buy the famous apple pies made by a Chinese nun who joined the community in China when she was 18. Now, at age 76, she bakes "for the glory of God and not me. If you really do work for God, it will keep you happy." The devotion and warmth of the sisters are what people remember and come back for.

Our Lady of Peace Retreat
3600 SW 170th Ave.
Beaverton, OR 97006
(503) 649-7127

Accommodations: *60 men, women, and children are accommodated in mainly singles with connecting baths; plain buildings, simple old-fashioned place; meals cafeteria-style with home cooking; community invites retreatants to join them for mass, morning, evening, and night prayer in their chapel; also a retreatants' chapel; 25 acres just off main street in Beaverton; special retreats for nursing mothers, mothers with toddlers, couples with babies (baby-sitters provided if wanted); AA retreats, summer catechetical program, private retreats, available for all groups to plan their own retreats or workshops; nice garden walk, open year-round; $30 a day.*

Directions: *All freeways approaching Portland have clearly indicated* BEAVERTON *signs. Follow these to Beaverton and proceed west on the Tualatin Valley Hwy. (Oregon No. 8). At 170th Ave. turn right (north) and enter the retreat parking lot at the next right turn.*

Shalom Prayer Center
Queen of Angels Monastery
Mount Angel, OR

The giant sequoia in front of the monastery was planted in 1893, and the 40 acres of beautiful grounds, along both sides of South Main Street, are lined with pin oaks and incense cedars. There is a bulge-eye catalpa, an American smoke, and a Kentucky coffee tree. Four American linden trees planted in 1903 border the walk to the north entrance. The monastery orchard contains apple, pear, prune, plum, cherry, and quince trees, as well as a grape arbor—a dazzling array of what will grow in this fertile section of Oregon.

The Benedictine sisters arrived here in 1882, and by 1887, at the behest of the German settlers, were teaching in a number of the local parish schools as well as building the central part of the red-brick monastery, which was completed in 1888. The north wing was added in 1903, the south wing in 1912. The reception room off the main entrance still retains the melancholy charm of those early days.

There are 45 sisters who live here and gather in the south wing chapel for morning, noon, and evening liturgy. Mass is said daily at 5:30 P.M. There are some private rooms in Howard Hall for women retreatants. The Shalom Prayer Center, a separate building across the lawn, has 15 rooms for men and women seeking "a place of prayer and peace." Spiritual direction and counseling are available on request.

There is a regular series of workshops and prayer meetings held in the Shalom Center. Some relate to the Church calendar; others are weekly meetings that examine prayer in everyday life. Workshops deal with Jungian psychology in an advanced Meyers-Briggs format. One or two weekend retreats are given each month on such topics as "Aging Gracefully," "Mothers and Daughters Together," and "Caregivers: A Time for Information and Mutual Support."

The sisters who live here are true examples of Benedictines responding to the needs of the times. In addition to offering warm hospitality through retreat work, they teach in schools and parishes, and work as nurses, counselors, chaplains, and parish associates. In 1957, they founded the Benedictine Nursing Center, which still derives its sense of purpose from the sisters. Some of the buildings on the grounds, formerly dormitories when there was a school here, have been turned into shelters for local farm and cannery migrant workers and their families.

Shalom Prayer Center
Queen of Angels Monastery
840 S. Main St.
Mount Angel, OR 97362
(503) 845-6773

Accommodations: *15 rooms with double or twin beds in the center for men and women, plus 15 more available in Howard Hall next door for women only; home-cooked meals; prayer 4 times daily in monastery and 2 times daily in retreat house; 40-acre grounds, work with sisters in garden, kitchen, wherever needed; apple orchards, cherries, berries on grounds; open year-round; $35–$40 a day.*

Directions: *I-5 to Woodburn/Silverton exit north of Salem; County Hwy. 214 to Mount Angel. Turn left after you cross over railroad tracks on Main St. Tallest tree in town (sequoia) in front of monastery on left.*

Tilikum Center for Retreats and Outdoor Ministries
Newberg, OR

In 1970 the Russell Baker family donated its 92-acre farm to a Christian group for camping and retreat purposes on an interdenominational basis. The former dairy farm has a 15-acre lake, meadows, and woods, and still has the look and feel of a working farm. Located in the Chehalem Valley seven miles from Newberg, the place offers a real opportunity to return to nature. Rabbits and goats still live in the barn, and horses and donkeys graze in the pasture, happy to receive attention from visitors. Canoes are available for exploring the lake, which ducks and beavers frequent; fishing is easy and pleasant along the grassy banks.

In 1975 the retreat became a part of nearby George Fox College, but it retains a full-time staff to perpetuate its function as a center for outdoor ministry. Throughout the year there are adult retreats, day camps for children, and Elderhostel groups. There is a multipurpose building in a stand of Douglas firs at the side of the lake. Built of logs and designed like an Indian longhouse, it is an activity center for large groups and is the location of the famous Tilikum salmon bakes.

The large, reconditioned farmhouse can accommodate 45 people with shared bathrooms. Eight Elderhostel groups were scheduled for 1991. Catholic, Lutheran, Baptist, Evangelical, and Bible study groups used the facility for weekend retreats in 1990. A program of day retreats is held by a master gardener who uses Scripture to relate to various areas of gardening and horticulture.

In 1986 a neighborhood one-room schoolhouse, from the turn of the century, was moved to the property and carefully restored. The authentic interior is furnished with period schoolroom desks and other memorabilia. It is often used for meetings and prayer services.

The name Tilikum, meaning "friend," is from the Chinook trade language used by Northwest Indian tribes who frequented the area before white settlement. The green pastures and quiet waters of Tilikum are a reminder of what a friend we have in nature, if we only take the time to notice.

Tilikum Center for Retreats and Outdoor Ministries
15321 NE N. Valley Rd.
Newberg, OR 97132
(503) 538-2763

Accommodations: *For men, women, and children, 45 beds with 2–9 per room in comfortably converted house; plans for space for 12 more couples and a hermitage in the woods for 2; homemade and nutritious family-style meals; cross-denominational organization, as is George Fox College, the Quaker College that owns the center; 92 acres, 15-acre lake, canoes galore, hiking trails, goats, mule "Molly June," bunnies, A-frame for solitary meditation, indoor and outdoor recreation from basketball to pool, fishing and volleyball, big swing, cable crossing, monthly Elderhostels; open year-round; $33 a day.*

Directions: *North of Salem take Brooks exit off I-5 and go left across freeway ½ mile to Hwy. 219 and turn right. Follow 219 North through St. Paul to Newberg. Going west in Newberg turn right (north) at intersection of Hwy. 99W and Hwy. 240 (CHEHALEM VALLEY sign). Follow Hwy. 240 for 5 miles. Turn right (north), leaving 240 at TILIKUM sign. After 1mile bear left at junction onto N. Valley Rd. Watch for sign on right in 1 mile.*

Oregon:
Other Places

Cerro Gordo, P.O. Box 569, **Cottage Grove,** OR 97424. (503) 942-7720

Chagdud Gonpa, 198 N. River Rd., **Cottage Grove,** OR 97424. (503) 942-8619

St. Benedict Lodge, 56630 N. Bank Rd., **McKenzie Bridge,** OR 97401. (503) 822-3572

Nestucca Sanctuary, **Pacific City,** OR 97135.

Loyola Retreat House, 3220 SE 43rd Ave., **Portland,** OR 97206. (503) 777-2225

Harbor Villa Retreat Center, P.O. Box 6, **Rockaway Beach,** OR 97136. (503) 355-2284

Aesculapia Wilderness Retreat, P.O. Box 301, **Wilderville,** OR 97543. (503) 476-0492

Man does not weave the web of life,
He is merely a strand in it.
Whatever he does to the web,
He does to himself.

CHIEF SEATTLE

Washington

CANADA

BRITISH COLUMBIA

VANCOUVER
ISLAND

Vancouver

WESTMINSTER ABBEY Mission

SALT SPRING CENTRE Ganges

Duncan
FAIRBURN FARM

Bellingham
Olga DOE BAY VILLAGE
Eastsound INDRALAYA

Victoria

IMMACULATE
HEART

Clinton
CHINOOK
LEARNING CENTER

Chelan
HOLDEN
VILLAGE

SPOKANE
RIVER

Spokane

Seattle STILL POINT
CONVENT OF ST. HELENA

BEAR TRIBE
MEDICINE
SOCIETY

Federal Way
REDEMPTORIST PALISADES RETREAT,
Tacoma VISITATION RETREAT CENTER

KAIROS
HOUSE OF
PRAYER

PACIFIC
OCEAN

Lacey
ST. MARTIN'S
ABBEY GUESTHOUSE

YAKIMA RIVER

Castle Rock
CLOUD
MOUNTAIN

COLUMBIA RIVER

Bear Tribe Medicine Society
Spokane, WA

Founded in 1970 by Sun Bear, an American Indian of Ojibway descent, this is a community of energetic, self-reliant people who share his vision and live together on 35 acres of Vision Mountain. The buildings are on the side of the rugged mountain looking across to the Spokane Indian reservation. The log longhouse was built in the early 1980s and serves as a central meeting and dining area as well as the residence of some members of the Bear Tribe. The community is self-supporting through book and magazine publishing and teaching programs throughout the year. There is a ten-day vision quest held here and at other locations in the United States and Europe about four times a year. It consists of earth-awareness exercises and ceremonies that help to open one's eyes and ears to Mother Earth. Many who attend the program go back to their daily lives with a deeper sense of aliveness, naturalness, and connection to all life.

Sun Bear, a noted author, lecturer, and medicine teacher, seeks to share the neglected wisdom of indigenous people who lived with great respect for the land. "In our technologically oriented society, we are starving for an earth connection," a spokesperson said. "The children of the oppressor are seeking the knowledge of the oppressed. Most religions put intellect on a pedestal and disregard the body, limiting and checking the emotions . . . don't deny them but seek a balance. Remember that it's one big circle; all living creatures are interrelated."

The philosophy here suggests that changes in our attitude toward the earth are necessary, and that these changes are ones that need to be made within. Those who survive will be prepared on *all* levels of their lives.

"The Earth is talking to us all the time," Sun Bear writes, "but most people have become deaf to her voice. When you begin your day as I do by thanking the Creator for the gift of life, you begin to regain your ability to hear the natural world around you."

Skilled persons who can contribute to a burgeoning spiritual family are invited to investigate the possibilities. Limited numbers of work-exchange arrangements for communal living are available.

Bear Tribe Medicine Society
P.O. Box 9167
Spokane, WA 99209
(509) 258-7755

Accommodations: *Camping on the land during programs for 30 men and women with outhouses and showers available; 3 meals a day using their garden produce, served at picnic tables outside; in winter, community shares meal responsibility in longhouse; sweat lodge, tepee, and the land used for ceremonies; contemplative meditation (looking out, not in); celebrations 4 times a year; Medicine Wheel gathering, Equinox Earth gathering, trip to ancient Mayan power places with Sun Bear, builder's school (6-week introduction to fundamentals of building), introductory apprentice program, vision quest, Sun Bear workshops; open year-round for community, programs June–September; visitor fee $20 a day, fee for 10-day program approximately $600.*

Directions: *Call or write for directions.*

Chinook Learning Center
Clinton, WA

The center is located on Whidby Island, a 20-minute car ferry ride from mainland Washington about an hour north of Seattle; or it can be approached from the north by crossing the bridge at Deception Pass, named by early explorers who were deceived into thinking this was the Northwest Passage to Europe. Part of the island network of Puget Sound in the Strait of Juan de Fuca, Whidby is the largest of the eight islands that make up Island County and one of only three that are inhabited. Although it is largely rural, there are a few small villages like Clinton that provide basic services.

Chinook Learning Center, a few miles outside Clinton, is on 72 acres of meadows and evergreen trees, a remote outpost that was, in the early 1900s, a homestead of Finnish farmers. In 1972, Vivienne and Fritz Hull acquired the property for use as a place to examine the basic question of why we are here. They were inspired by the 6th-century Celtic Christian monastic school on Iona, an island off the coast of Scotland, where thousands were drawn for a special kind of education and training and then were deeply influential in Europe. Like Iona, Chinook seeks to be a center for study and teaching to create an understanding of the meaning and purpose of life, linking humanity and the earth and the concomitant spiritual values.

Chinook offers year-round courses, workshops, retreats, conferences, and training programs in religion, ecology, psychology, and cultural change. There is room for 20 people in a variety of accommodations. The reconditioned farmhouse and "Granny's," a house that was donated and moved to the property, have comfortable rooms with indoor plumbing and kitchens. Two rustic cabins, heated with woodburning stoves, are set in the woods. There is a community bathhouse and outhouses nearby. Larger groups make use of the open meadows for camping. Private retreatants are accommodated according to space available and can use the kitchen to prepare their own food.

A small group of caretakers lives here and is aided by members of the Chinook community, who live nearby and help to keep the facility in good repair and functioning smoothly. There is a great appreciation for the land and the life-style demonstrated by the rustic neatness of the buildings and the well-tended flower and vegetable gardens. A number of marked trails wind through the second-growth fir and cedars.

Chinook is an Indian word meaning "warm wind blowing," describing a warm winter wind that suggests the coming of spring. The name of this remote retreat expresses its raison d'être perfectly: like a fresh wind, summoning people to meet the challenges confronting all of us to work for a better world. "Nothing is outside the arena of what we call spiritual," Vivienne Hull writes. "Understanding that all of life is sacred changes your economics, your politics, and your relationships."

Chinook Learning Center
P.O. Box 57
Clinton, WA 98236
(206) 221-3153

Accommodations: Can accommodate 20 men, women, and children indoors using the Farmhouse, 2 cabins, and "Granny's"; summer camping for up to 100; delicious, hearty, vegetarian meals for groups or programs the center runs, use of kitchen if no groups there; Sunday service at Dodge Building in town; 1st Sunday of each month is a children's service at the Farmhouse; many spiritual traditions from Celtic Christian to Native American earth-based paths; seasonal festivals throughout the year; sauna, hiking trails, 72 acres of fir and cedar forest and meadows, great swamp; wonderful gardens; open year-round; $25–$30 per person with breakfast, $40–$45 per couple; dinner $5 each when available; work/exchange retreat $15 a night plus 4 hours work.

Directions: I-5 North from Seattle to Mukilteo exit and follow signs to ferry. Take ferry to Clinton. Drive from ferry onto Hwy. 525 North, a 4-lane, then 2-lane, road, and turn left onto Campbell to stop sign. Go ½ mile beyond and see sign and drive on left.

Cloud Mountain Retreat Center
Castle Rock, WA

Carpenter and artist David Branscomb and wife, Anna, a systems analyst, were looking for a way to work with spiritual friends. Their meditation practice—she trained in Vipassana and he in Zen—helped them to decide to use land that had been a gift as a place where Buddhist groups and individuals could come to meditate and study. Since 1984, the center has made the facilities available to Buddhist groups regardless of tradition or sect. In cooperation with the Northwest Dharma Association, there are regularly scheduled retreats, classes, sittings, and special events throughout the year, and private retreatants are welcome.

The charming wooden buildings are on five acres of sloping, forested land and were sited according to the earth's energy flow. There is no electricity. Light is provided by propane lamps as easy to use as striking a match; heating comes from woodstoves and propane heaters. Communal showers with hot water are in a separate building; there are a few flush toilets as well as outhouses. There are accommodations for 34 people in two buildings, some in private rooms, others dormitory-style with two to five beds per room. A large dining room in the main house offers three vegetarian meals a day. Guests help to clean up after meals. Tea and fruit are available throughout the day. Retreatants should bring their own bedding, pillow, and towels. A flashlight is essential.

There are two meditation halls on the property as well as a pond, garden, greenhouse, and a sauna. The buildings, each in its own woodland setting, are reached by neat pathways. At night, the overhanging trees merge into the dark like an Ad Reinhardt painting. The occasional squawk of a roosting peacock lends a mysterious air. On a clear day, the snow-capped peak of Mount Rainier can be seen 50 miles north.

Cloud Mountain Retreat Center
373 Agren Rd.
P.O. Box 807
Castle Rock, WA 98611
(206) 274-4859

Accommodations: 34 beds for men, women, and children in 2 heated (with propane and wood), rustic, but comfortable sleeping buildings with 2–5 in a room, and several private rooms in another building; central bathhouse with hot water and flush toilets in addition to outhouses on this beautiful wooded property; bring own bedding, towels, and flashlight; 3 delicious vegetarian meals a day; private retreats and retreats with meditation teachers; walking paths, organic garden, greenhouse, sauna, small lake, fish pond, view of Mount Rainier and Mount St. Helens; resident cats, chickens, goldfish, peacocks; guests help with meal preparation and cleanup; open year-round; $30 a day.

Directions: From Seattle, go south on I-5 (about 2¼ hrs) and take Exit 59 (Vader-Ryderwood). You will intersect Hwy. 506 at the stop sign. 1 hour north of Portland on I-5 to Exit 59 (Veder-Ryderwood exit, which is beyond Castle Rock exit). Sharp cutback under bridge (west side) to Hwy. 506. Left on 506 and go 3 miles to crossroads and Rte. 411. Left on 411 and go 2½ miles to Agren Rd. (just beyond overpass for railroad). Turn right on Agren for ¼ mile and watch for mailbox on left, across from red barn.

Convent of St. Helena
Seattle, WA

This convent is part of the Order of St. Helena, a religious community of women in the Episcopal church that lives a contemporary version of traditional monasticism. They came to this quiet neighborhood in the Capitol Hill district of Seattle in 1982 to be a focal point for serving the Pacific Northwest. The charming, spacious, Tudor-style residence is described as "neither monastic nor elegant but a neutral space with donated furniture." It is well kept and cared for by four sisters who see hospitality as one of their important responsibilities. The primary mission is a prayerful life within the community. They meet four times a day in the basement chapel beginning at 7 A.M. followed by Eucharist, again at noon, then Vespers at 5:30 P.M. and Compline at 7:30.

There are four double rooms for guests who desire a peaceful atmosphere in a quiet, supportive setting. Guests structure their own time and are welcome at all prayer services. Pick-up breakfast and lunch are available in the kitchen. The community and guests share an evening meal in the dining room. One of the sisters is available for discussion if requested.

The Order of St. Helena was founded in 1945 and has its mother house in Vails Gate, NY, 60 miles north of New York City. The community has 18 life-professed members and 5 in training; other convents are in Manhattan and Augusta, GA. The members of the order make vows of poverty, chastity, and obedience to God's will as perceived through their own insight as well as the insights of others.

The sisters are available to conduct retreats and for spiritual direction. They preach and teach in parishes and do volunteer work with the handicapped. There is a regular schedule of quiet days and evenings and retreats at the convent. This is a welcoming atmosphere that offers a place of prayer, retreat, and renewal.

Convent of St. Helena
1114 21st Ave. E.
Seattle, WA 98112
(206) 325-2830

Accommodations: *4 gracious double guest rooms with hand-crocheted afghans, for men and women, in this lovely Seattle neighborhood; home-cooked dinner served in dining room with community and breakfast and lunch provided; 4 Offices daily and Eucharist 5 times weekly; beautiful enamel work by Sister Ellen Stephen; blooming plants and garden; neighborhood walks with views of water; closed August; suggested donation: $25 a day.*

Directions: *From the south on I-5 to Madison St. exit. Right on Madison to 19th Ave. Left on 19th to Prospect St., then right on Prospect to 21st Ave. Left on 21st to second house on right.*

Doe Bay Village Resort
Olga, WA

Doe Bay is located on Orcas Island, part of the San Juan Islands off the Washington coast, and can be reached by regular ferry service from Anacortes, WA, or Sidney BC. It is not unusual to see the sleek black backs and high dorsal fins of the Orcas (the small whales for which the island is named) gliding offshore. From the ferry landing, a two-lane road follows a semicircular route for 26 miles to the southern tip of the kidney-shaped island. There on the beach at Doe Bay is the meditative, rustic retreat where, as one writer described, "You can't get much farther away from it all without falling into the water."

In the early 1900s, Doe Bay Village was founded as a freight terminus for island produce. The wooden general store and post office, constructed in 1908, were placed on the National Register of Historic Places in 1986. Through the years, the 60-acre site has had a varied history—as an art colony, health spa, and New Age commune called the Polarity Institute. The current stewards see the evolution toward a communiversity—a center for meditation, lectures, and benevolent events.

There is no specific religious affiliation here but a great appreciation for the beauty of the setting and a casual and warm welcome for those who visit. Accommodations range from double rooms with showers and central kitchens in secluded duplex buildings to rustic cottages and cabins with nearby bathrooms. There are hostel-type buildings with dormitories and a large retreat house for 20 with a meeting room, kitchen, and bathrooms. Bedding is supplied for cabins and cottages but others should bring sleeping bags. Campers are welcome and there are hookups for recreation vehicles.

There are open-air mineral baths, the water heated to 106 degrees, with an adjacent cold pool overlooking the bay. Cedar, fir, and mountain ash trees are silhouetted against the water.

From the shoreline, you can observe otters swimming in Otter Cove, and looking across the serene waters to the islands beyond makes clear what a young staff member said: "No one ever leaves Doe Bay; they may physically but their heart doesn't."

Doe Bay Village Resort
Star Route 86
Olga, WA 98279
(206) 376-2291 or 376-4755

Accommodations: *For men, women, and children, 22 rooms and cabins, including one called "Children's," which comes with a fenced yard, and "Treehouse," which has one bed; 8 hostel beds, and a retreat house that sleeps 20 and is secluded from the rest of the accommodations, plus 60 beautiful acres for camping; vegetarian meals available in-season and weekends from café that overlooks the water; guest kitchen and general store available year-round; meditation trail, "Contemplation Point," 2 outdoor mineral springs, hot tubs, wood-fired cedar sauna overlooking Otter Cove; volleyball, badminton, Ping-Pong; abundant bird and sea life; sea kayaking with experienced island kayak guides $25; adjoins wildlife refuge; whale watching; open year-round; $63.50 cabin with kitchen and bathroom, $38.50 a day European-style sleeping huts, $12.50 hostel beds, $8.50 campsites, $2 per animal a day; work-trade program—bring tents in summer.*

Directions: *Anacortes Ferry to Orcas Island. Left off ferry and follow signs on Horseshoe Hwy. to Olga through Moran State Park. Then follow* DOE BAY *signs (22 miles, 40 minutes).*

Fairburn Farm
Duncan, BC

Nestled in the Cowichan Valley, on Vancouver Island north of Victoria and outside the town of Duncan, the 130 acres of Fairburn Farm face the Koksilah Ridge to the west. The rolling, heavily wooded hills surrounding the property serve as a natural buffer to the outside world. Situated at the end of a county road, the farm buildings look down and across open meadows and pastures dotted with grazing sheep—a peaceful and bucolic setting.

In 1955, Mollie and Jack Archer acquired the farm, and through the years these pioneers of conservation created a model of self-sufficiency using organic means. Darrel Archer and his English-born wife, Anthea, still follow that lead and raise lambs commercially; milk the cows; tend the chickens; cultivate oats, barley, and wheat, as well as garden vegetables for family and guests. They churn butter from their own milk and use flour from homegrown wheat for bread and scones. Jams and jellies come from their own fruit trees, eggs from their chickens; the rhubarb pie made fresh from the garden is world-class. "It takes a couple of days for guests to unwind," Anthea said. "Then after a week, we practically have to pack for them to leave."

The tastefully refurbished 100-year-old farmhouse has a parlor and dining room reminiscent of an English country house. There are six guest rooms on the second floor, each with private baths. Meals are arranged according to guests' needs. There is a separate self-contained cottage behind the farmhouse with kitchen and bedrooms, available on a weekly basis.

Trails follow the creek that winds through the property and the lanes along the fenced fields are pleasant to stroll. The large front porch is a comfortable place to sit and look out on the pastoral setting and commune with nature.

Fairburn Farm
3310 Jackson Rd. RR 7
Duncan, BC V9L 4W4
Canada
(604) 746-4637

Accommodations: *6 comfortable and pleasant queen and twin rooms with private baths, looking out on this beautiful farm and mountains beyond, for men, women, and children; hearty and delicious breakfast included; approximately $10 for lunch, $19 for dinner using homegrown organic food from garden and their own lambs, churned butter, scones, own wheat for bread (special menus can be arranged to suit needs of guests); daily farm tasks; milking cows, feeding animals, collecting eggs; seasonally: sheep shearing, haymaking, combining, sawmilling, harvesting the garden and orchard; hiking on 130 acres, swimming and fishing in clear mountain stream, kayaks, horseshoes, badminton, archery, mountain bikes, relaxing on front porch or in front of fireplace; open Easter–Halloween; $66–$102 a day for 2 people per room with breakfast; additional guests beyond 2 can be accommodated in some rooms for $15 a day; cottage available too.*

Directions: *From Victoria, BC, take Hwy. 1 toward Duncan. After coming down from mountain into Mill Bay go approximately 6 miles and watch for Payless Gas on left, firehall on right, and set of stoplights. Turn left at lights on Koksilah Rd. and travel approximately 2 miles (beyond bridge and river) to Jackson Rd. (partially hidden by bushes). Turn left on Jackson and follow straight, onto dirt road, to end.*

Holden Village
Chelan, WA

If retreats were judged on remoteness and inaccessibility, Holden Village would be at the top of the list. The adventure unfolds in stages starting from the village of Chelan at the southern tip of Lake Chelan, which lies within an 80-mile-long glacial valley near Washington's geographic center, and the ferry for the 16-mile trip to Holden's dock at Lucerne. A few miles above Chelan, both sides of the narrow lake become part of the National Forest Preserve and there are no roads—only trails for grazing deer and white-coated mountain goats that climb the high ridges. In some places the rugged shoreline is fjordlike, and the snow-capped peaks of the northern Cascade Mountains rise more than 7,000 feet in the distance. A bus from Holden Village meets the ferry and transports guests the last 12 miles up the single-lane road deep into the rugged terrain to the base of Copper Mountain.

Holden Village was built in the 1930s as a settlement for copper miners and their families with all the conveniences of small-town life. The mine ceased operation in 1957 and the property was offered for sale. Wes Prieb, then in Alaska, read about the closing and wrote to inquire the asking price, which was $100,000. The next year he wrote again and got the same response. In 1960, while a student at the Lutheran Bible Institute in Seattle, he wrote again. This time the reply came by telephone that the mining company was donating the property to the Lutheran Bible Institute and asked that Wes be responsible. That summer when a group came to evaluate the property, one church official advised, "No more camps are needed by the Lutheran church"; another said, "Holden should be turned over to the U.S. government as a center for training spies." In the fall, when Wes was living at Holden as a caretaker he went one afternoon into the auditorium and prayed that Holden be taken over and rebuilt, and every stone and timber there be dedicated to the honor and glory of God, that many people would come to help, and that young people would find Christ here and emerge with changed lives. In that spirit, Holden has been rebuilt and is now a thriving renewal community where 70 men, women, and children live year-round. Some come for a few months in the summer, some for a year, taking a sabbatical where they can step aside and evaluate where they are and where they're going. The community celebrates the wide variety of gifts and skills that people of all races, cultures, and beliefs can bring. Hospitality is a central theme, for the people of Holden Village feel that this wonderfully remote and inspiring place is not to be owned but shared.

There are plain but comfortable guest rooms available throughout the year. Meals are family-style in the large dining room, which is quickly transformed into a theater for an evening's festivities.

Vespers are held daily, and community members with the resident chaplain take turns being responsible for the service. Aside from the busy summer schedule, there are weekend and mid-week retreats throughout the year that offer a time of study and interaction around specific spiritual topics.

Holden Village
Chelan, WA 98816

Accommodations: Room for 250 men, women, and children in comfortable, simple rooms for 2–4 in old hotel and other buildings; tasty, family-style meals with limited use of meat, and 1 meal a week of bread or rice or potatoes only, to reflect world hunger concerns; daily worship attendance required at Vespers and Eucharist on Sunday; hiking, climbing, fishing, snowshoeing, cross-country skiing; famous pool hall, library, bookstore, craft and pottery area, museum, sauna, bowling alley; programs for children and adults all summer; volunteer staff positions available for those 18 and over, from 3 weeks to 2 years, depending on job; open year-round; $32–$40 a day depending on length of stay and age of children.

Directions: Only by boat from the town of Chelan. A bus from the village will meet you at the landing. There is no telephone, so arrangements and deposit must be organized by letter. Good place to stay in Lake Chelan is the Parkway Motel, (509) 682-2822. If you stay there coming and going you can leave your car with them, and they will deliver and pick you up at the ferry.

Immaculate Heart Retreat House
Spokane, WA

Just a few miles south of the center of Spokane, on a 50-acre site amid the hills of the Moran Prairie near Tower Mountain, this Catholic retreat was built in the late 1950s. Appealing to the independent, pioneer spirit of the people of Spokane, the first non-Indian settlement in the Pacific Northwest, Bishop Bernard Topel carefully articulated the importance of having a center in the diocese for renewal and spiritual refreshment. Fireside meetings were held in private homes and parish halls throughout the diocese to enlist the support of those who would most benefit. The result was a classic example of religious and lay cooperation. Since the first retreat was hosted in February 1959, tens of thousands of people have spent time here either in groups or as individual retreatants. Parishes use it as a place for training programs and as an outreach to Native Americans. There is a great variety of courses going on throughout the year, including a series of 8-day and 30-day retreats and an AA and codependency program. Private directed retreats can be accommodated at any time.

There are tidy, efficient single rooms for 110 to 120 people. Each has a sink and toilet, and each floor has separate shower rooms for men and women. Meals are served cafeteria-style in the main-floor dining room, where coffee, tea, and snacks are always available. There are two daily morning masses in the chapel at 7 and 11.

The large belltower, completed in 1959, was designed as a stylized lily, expressing the words "To Jesus through Mary." The tall spire forms an M for Mary and the stamens of the lily form a cross. Named after the Immaculate Heart of Mary, the center has a special devotion to her and celebrations are held on days that coincide with significant events relating to her. The rosary terrace, a large oval 500 feet in circumference, has a shrine to Our Lady of Fatima in the center of the grotto.

In addition to three chapels in the main building, there are two elegant, small wooden chapels sitting off by themselves that are perfect for individual prayer and meditation. The Nazareth House, a quadriplex guesthouse on the south side of the property, has self-contained units suitable for private retreats. The grounds are spacious and easy to walk on. There are tranquil views to the south and west over the prairie.

Immaculate Heart Retreat House
S. 6910 Ben Burr Rd.
Spokane, WA 99223
(509) 448-1224

Accommodations: *For 110–120 men, women, and children, mainly singles with private toilet and sink in main house, Earth House, Nazareth House, White House, and Red House; cafeteria-style meals, home-cooked, tasty and attractive; mass twice daily; lovely walks and gardens in this countryside setting with little prayer chapels on property in addition to 3 chapels in main building; closed last 2 weeks of August; suggested donation: $50 a day (rates for groups available).*

Directions: *Right off I-90 at Colfax (Exit 279), 5 miles on Hwy. 195 to Hatch Rd., left up hill, right on 57th Ave., east 2 miles; cross Palouse Hwy. intersection at stop sign, go east ½ block, and right on S. Ben Burr Rd. for 1 mile to retreat on right.*

Indralaya
Eastsound, WA

The 76 acres of this remote retreat are on Orcas Island, at the end of a long, unpaved road where almost a mile of shorefront borders the edge of the property. The heavily wooded site has a three-acre meadow and orchard inhabited by families of wild rabbits. Facing the meadow is the community center, a large inviting structure built of unfinished wood where the kitchen-dining area and meeting room with stone fireplace is the hub of activity. Meals are served buffet-style, taken to long tables or outside in good weather, and each person is responsible for cleanup. Hot drinks are available throughout the day. The large windows at the back of the building look out to the woods and water below.

Around the meadow, tucked beneath tall cedars and firs, are rustic cabins, each in its own setting. The cabins are furnished with bed, table, and chair, and heated with a woodburning stove; the woodpiles are easily accessible. For those cabins that do not have plumbing, there are separate bathhouses for men and women.

Indralaya is a Sanskrit word suggesting the home or resting place of the spiritual forces in nature. In 1927, the Theosophical Society acquired the property as a place where members and friends could come to investigate the workings of nature and man, to encourage the study of science and comparative religions. Theosophy, called the ageless wisdom or wisdom religion, is concerned with that which is hidden, not obvious. It deals with nature's unseen processes and laws that stand behind and beyond science and is concerned with living harmoniously in the world with nature and all beings. Consistent with this approach, vegetarianism and harmlessness to all life are practiced.

There is a traditional summer camp during July and August oriented to families and campers of all ages with a morning lecture and an evening campfire. During the spring, fall, and winter there are work weekends when visitors help with grounds maintenance, tree pruning, and cabin rehabilitation. There are other weekends for seminars and workshops on topics of Theosophical interest. Private retreatants who share the espoused values here can be accommodated.

A trail winds above and along the shoreline leading to benches and grassy slopes that afford secluded outlooks across the bay. Attracted by the isolation and quiet of the island, bald eagles nest in the tall trees. Loons and otters—those solitary creatures—are also frequently seen.

Indralaya
Rte. 1, Box 86
Eastsound, WA 98245
(206) 376-4526

Accommodations: *30 cabins for 2 or more men, women, and children, some with plumbing, the rest with facilities nearby; bring your own sheets, towels, flashlight; tasty lacto-vegetarian meals served in large community dining room; summer camp for 2 months opened each season by Dora Kunz with a meditational retreat; she also teaches therapeutic touch in June; a variety of programs during season with a morning discussion in apple orchard on science, philosophy, religion, ethics, creativity, healing; outstanding spiritual library; 76 acres of lawn, woods, and waterfront with hiking trails, beach, badminton; abundant wildlife, from bald eagles overhead to rabbits everywhere; no smoking has been allowed on the property since 1927, except in your own car; open year-round; $35–$50 a day per person, off-season meditational retreat with work exchange is $25 a day with own food.*

Directions: *Take ferry from Anacortes, WA, to Orcas Island. Follow road to left as you leave ferry and drive 7½ miles. Just past golf course (and blue-and-white class reunion sign) is* INDRALAYA/ORCAS ISLAND FOUNDATION *sign. Turn right onto dirt road to camp at end of road.*

Kairos House of Prayer
Spokane, WA

This 27 acres of wooded hilltop is a sanctuary for those seeking peace and quiet. At the end of a private lane, 2,300 feet above sea level, there are splendid views to the east and west. A large house, barn, and seven hermitages are nestled among Ponderosa pines and glacier rocks.

In the 1970s, with the encouragement and blessing of Bishop Bernard Topel of Spokane, Sister Florence Leone established a place of contemplative experience. Following the advice of Brother David Steindl-Rast, who suggested a more experiential approach, she studied Buddhist meditation and yoga, to enlarge the traditional form of prayer. She realized that Benedictine monasticism was experiential and that centering prayer was a part of Catholicism centuries ago. She practiced more meditative sitting and realized that "East" and "West" are only in our minds. The aim is to bring everything together, to move into a realm where there is neither gentile nor Jew, servant nor free, black nor white, red nor yellow. Spiritual life is part of the whole experience as a person. We need to cultivate the Eastern concept of letting go—with the emphasis on being rather than doing—tap into yoga breathing techniques, and concentrate on where we are going.

Taking the Greek work *kairos,* which means "the present time, that is—now," as a guiding directive, this contemplative community has established a rhythm of prayer, work, and study. They come together for meditation at 7:30 A.M., 11:30 A.M., and 5 P.M. There is daily Eucharist. A priest comes twice a week to say mass. There are one-day and weeklong retreats where individuals can stay in the hermitages, which are very comfortable, private, and overlook the valley. The wind sighs through the pines and the night sky is dazzling. Silent vegetarian meals are served in the kitchen in the main house.

People who come here are grateful for the very existence of somewhere they can reconnect with themselves, reconnoiter, and explore the meaning of life. Many people return regularly, like coming home to a welcoming spirit, a climate of safety and security.

Kairos House of Prayer
W. 1714 Stearns Rd.
Spokane, WA 99208
(509) 466-2187

Accommodations: *9 private rooms in main house and barn, and 7 hermitages, all comfortable, with electricity; hermitages have Porta-potty (or short walk to shared baths), hot plates, refrigerator, and bottled water; meals with community, eaten in silence in main house; daily liturgy or service; morning and evening meditation; centering meditation, deep relaxation and concentration, breathing methods, physical postures; 27 acres and country roads for walking; open year-round; $25 a day.*

Directions: *Exit 281 (Newport-Colville) from I-90. Drive north on Division St. (U.S. 2-395) Continue straight on 395 approximately 10 miles. Turn left on Dartford Rd. (across from Wandermere Country Club) and go 7/10 mile to Hazard Rd. and turn left; go 1¼ miles to Stearns Rd. and turn left, then 1/10 mile and turn right. KAIROS and RED BARN RANCHETTE signs will be on your right as you proceed up drive to Kairos to big brown barn on left and brick house on right.*

The Redemptorist Palisades Retreat
Federal Way, WA

Looking across to Maury Island, this Catholic retreat sits 100 feet above Puget Sound where submarines and container ships, coast guard vessels, and pleasure boats glide by. The 35 acres of grounds have 700 feet of tidal beach, which can be reached by a steep stairway. Visitors can wander serenely along the shore and examine, among other things, an old wooden barge, the *Tacoma*, beached years ago.

In 1955 the Redemptorists were asked to build a retreat house for men as a counterpart to the one run by sisters down the road (see page 200). While remaining faithful to their mission over the years, they have increased their ministry to include high school students, Charismatic renewal, single parents, and directed retreats for men and women.

The large, T-shaped building sits on a high point, and the picture windows of the dining room and the adjoining lounge look out over the water. Meals are served cafeteria-style and are memorable for quality and quantity. There are 48 comfortably furnished private rooms on two levels, each with a toilet and sink. There are separate shower rooms for men and women on each floor. The rooms are named after saints and great spiritual leaders such as Mahatma Gandhi and Thomas Merton, Martin Luther King and Moses, a salute to the retreat's ecumenical outreach. Mass is said daily in the large chapel.

Since 1987, a family of bald eagles has lived in the tall pines at the edge of the property. There are trails through the woods, and outdoor stations of the cross, but as one brother pointed out, "Those who come are mainly looking for peace and quiet, not activity."

The small community of Redemptorists who live here and manage the center's programs are frequently asked about the vocation of being a brother, a calling that has a unique identity, purpose, and contribution that apparently is not always easily understood. One brother provides the perfect explanation: "I am a male nun."

The Redemptorist Palisades Retreat
4700 SW Dash Point Rd.
P.O. Box 3739
Federal Way, WA 98063
(206) 927-9621

Accommodations: *48 lovely private bedrooms (32 with double beds) and private baths with view of Puget Sound or gardens; separate house with 4 bedrooms can accommodate 8 men and women; delicious and hearty meals in nice dining room overlooking sound; daily mass; 35 acres; 5 bald eagles, stairs to beach, woods, trails; open year-round (January–April, men's retreat weekends; May–December, open to nonprofit groups, religious, private retreatants); $45 a day.*

Directions: *I-5 to Exit 143. Take SW 320 through Seatac Mall to end (past golf course). Right on 47th St., 5 blocks to stop sign, and left on Dash Point Rd. Watch immediately for sign on right.*

St. Martin's Abbey Guesthouse
Lacey, WA

On the 350-acre campus of St. Martin's College there is a charming brick building, used as a guesthouse, at the edge of the large playing field, just a short distance from the abbey church. There are 8 double rooms, comfortably furnished with twin beds, that are available for visitors to spend time in spiritual reflection. In a separate parlor hot drinks are always available, and meals are taken in the student dining room in the basement of Old Main nearby.

St. Martin's Abbey was founded in 1895 by Benedictine monks who came from Minnesota at the request of the bishop of Seattle to minister to German settlers. St. Martin's College was started as a grammar school and by 1900 college-level courses were added. In 1940, the liberal arts school became fully accredited. There are now more than 500 students, and about 150 live on the south side of the campus.

Only three miles from Olympia, the state capital of Washington, the abbey setting retains a rural atmosphere, a buffer zone of tranquil open fields, surrounded by full growth pine and fir trees. The huge cone of Mount Rainier is visible on the horizon.

The monks meet daily in the church for morning, noon, and evening sung prayer, and mass is celebrated during the week at 5 P.M., in the morning on weekends. Guests are welcome to attend all services. The fine details of the church are worth close inspection—from the intricately carved doors to the superb wooden statues and the lectern in the form of an eagle. Banners hang from the high walls behind the altar and just meet the tops of the windows—a most unusual and stunning feature. Concerts and lectures are held in the church periodically throughout the year. There are no formal retreat programs, but a monk is available for consultation. Visitors are left to their own devices to enjoy the peaceful setting and to roam the meadows and unspoiled woods.

The abbey was named after the 4th-century Italian soldier-saint who cut his cloak in half to give to a freezing beggar. The abbey and the college foster an educational attitude of creativity and originality in thinking with a strong sense of values in personal and social responsibility.

St. Martin's Abbey Guesthouse
5300 Pacific Ave. SE
Lacey, WA 98503
(206) 438-4457 or 491-4700

Accommodations: 16 twin beds in 8 rooms for men and women in this very pleasant guesthouse with parlor; tasty meals in student cafeteria for families; men alone dine with monks in refectory adjoining; prayer in church 4 times daily; church and monastery filled with lovely art, banners, windows, sculpture, gates; 350 acres of campus and grounds with view of Mount Rainier; tennis, field sports; beautiful new local library nearby; open year-round; $25 a day.

Directions: I-5 from the south to exit 108, right at light (College St.) and left at next light into St. Martin's Abbey Rd. to large red brick building to check in at information center/switchboard. From the north, take I-5 to Exit 109, go right on Martin Way and left at the first stoplight onto College St. Follow College St. to second stoplight and take a left into St. Martin's campus to check in as above.

Salt Spring Centre
Ganges, BC

The center is located on Salt Spring Island, in the Strait of Georgia just off the southeastern coast of Vancouver Island. Salt Spring is one of the Southern Gulf Islands, 20 miles long and 8 miles wide, and can be reached by ferry from the mainland and Vancouver Island. Settled in the 1850s, the few small villages at key shore points are picturesque hubs for the largely agricultural economy. It was to this tranquil setting that followers of Baba Hari Dass came in 1981 and purchased 69 acres of forest and meadows in the heart of the island, near the town of Ganges.

The center is a place for education in the broadest sense. It has a grade school for children from grades 1 through 7 and regular programs for adult study focusing on the development of positive qualities of character, creativity, and practical and productive skills in the context of spiritual growth. The community of eight adults and four children who live here, joined by another 20 members who live nearby, are dedicated to the ideals of Ashtanga Yoga. This is an ancient eightfold system, including meditation and postures familiar to many as hatha yoga, and scriptural study, the study and practice of nonpossessiveness, truthfulness, harmony, contentment, and simple peaceful living, all with the aim of realizing truth.

The main method of Salt Spring is service to others, that is seen as a means for reducing self-interest and gaining higher spiritual awareness, thus attempting to transcend the limitations of the individual and the group.

The center of activities is the Heritage House, a turn-of-the-century wooden house with a homelike atmosphere. The large meeting room with oak floors and stained-glass windows is warm and comfortable. The dining room is adjacent—a bright room where meals are served buffet-style, prepared by community members who rotate responsibility. Guest rooms for 20 are in this rambling structure.

The center is open to those who wish to examine and experience community life and work toward common goals. While personal skills are appreciated, the most important trait is a willingness to share in helping and learning. The spirit here follows the path of Baba Hari Dass (see Mount Madonna Center, page 62), who suggests, "Work honestly, meditate every day, meet people without fear, and play."

The Salt Spring Centre
355 Blackburn Rd.
Salt Spring Island
Mail: Box 1133, Ganges, BC V0S 1E0
Canada
(604) 537-2326

Accommodations: *For 20 men, women, and children, comfortable rooms for 2–4; isolation cabin for those with particular practice or path; tenting facilities for summer guests; tasty vegetarian meals; Sunday gathering with meditation; devotion, and singing; Monday night yoga; Friday A.M. Bhagavad Gita class; 69 acres of cedar forest, wild meadows, orchard, organic gardens for walking or helping, nature trail along creek; wood sauna; women's health weekends, ayurvedic weekend; Ramayana production, a major event each summer with fabulous costumes and music; open year-round except for Christmas; $40–$55 a day per person, or weekend programs $195–$225.*

Directions: *Convenient ferry access to Salt Spring Island is available from Vancouver (Tsawwassen), Vancouver Island (Swartz Bay & Crofton) and Anacortes, WA. For ferry schedules, call: Vancouver—(604) 669-1211; Anacortes—(206) 293-8166. Once on Salt Spring Island follow Fulford-Ganges Hwy. through town to Blackburn Rd. Turn right and watch for sign for center on left in ¼ mile.*

Still Point
A Center for Spirituality
Seattle, WA

On a quiet street in the Capitol Hill district of Seattle, a spacious, charming house is the communal home of a group of Catholic sisters. Originally, they belonged to different congregations but found they all shared a similar vision: to help others to grow spiritually, and by so doing increase their own spiritual growth.

Founded in 1974 as part of the House of Prayer movement, the concept of this spiritual center has become clearer and more precise: "Having a center place within yourself out of which you move in the world with love and peace and serenity," the director explained, "we have a home where we live that, so others can come to learn how." The center's goal is to foster contemplative living while maintaining an awareness of changing spiritual needs.

The sisters have four guest rooms with shared baths that are available for private retreatants. Visitors feel it is "like coming home" to a caring house, a place of peace, safety, and security. Guests help themselves to breakfast and lunch in the kitchen. There is an evening meal with the community served graciously, as though at a favorite relative's home for dinner. The community comes together daily for prayer at noon. There are also three churches where mass is said daily within walking distance.

The sisters hold a regular series of ongoing classes, such as the practice of centering prayer using Father Thomas Keating's video series, single days of reflection on topical Church holy days and periods, seminars on healing and motherhood, and the 12-step series. They hold workshops on dreams and journal writing, Meyers-Briggs profiles, and cosponsor an Enneagram workshop with the Lutheran Social Services. They are pleased to report that their guests are about half Protestant, half Catholic; 98 percent are laypeople, and 80 percent are women.

The house faces east with a commanding view of Lake Washington and the Cascade Mountains beyond. The neighborhood is pleasant and convenient. A few blocks west, buses run regularly to the city center, or guests can walk through one of the country's most livable cities and enjoy the views of the water.

Note: As this book was going to press, Still Point announced that it was looking for new premises, so check well in advance for details of the new location.

Still Point
A Center for Spirituality
2333 13th Ave. E.
Seattle, WA 98102
(206) 322-8006

Accommodations: *4 comfortable rooms for men and women in this pleasant house; home-cooked meals eaten with community; community prayer daily; located in pretty Seattle neighborhood looking out to water; there is walking in nearby park, and a trail to the arboretum; this is an urban retreat center; open year-round; $40 a day.*

Directions: *I-5 to Exit 168A Lakeview-Roanoke). Turn left at stop sign and go straight up hill with no turn. This becomes Harvard, then curves and becomes E. Miller. There is a light at 10th and Miller. Go 2 more blocks to Seattle Prep. School and turn right on 11th around parking lot, then left on E. Miller, which curves and becomes E. 13th. Still Point is the yellow house, second from corner.*

Visitation Retreat Center
Federal Way, WA

Located on a bluff looking across Dumas Bay to Puget Sound and west to the Olympic Mountains, the Catholic Sisters of the Visitation completed building their monastery–retreat house in 1958. These contemplative nuns wear a modified dress–habit and black veil with a white band, and perform a dual role. Their chief occupation is prayer, but they also host weekend retreats ten months of the year for women of the archdiocese of Seattle. Parishes in the diocese return each year on the same weekend. The sisters keep an elaborate file of those who have attended in the past and assign the rooms accordingly: one year a view of the water, and the next of the grounds.

There are 40 single rooms, comfortable and clean, each with a sink and toilet. Communal showers are down the hall. Excellent meals are available in the dining room. Visiting priests and deacons serve as retreat directors.

The sisters balance their gracious hospitality with five daily prayer sessions: 7 A.M., 4:30 and 8:15 P.M. are sung; the Office is read at 11:30 A.M. and 1:15 P.M. Daily mass is at 7:15 A.M. Visitors and retreatants are welcome at these services, which are held in the chapel. The gentle voices of the sisters are calm and soothing.

The grounds around the single, large building are spacious and exceptionally well-kept. It is a pleasure to walk on the lawns at the edge of the bluff.

These endearing women are serious yet playful. One recounted a community decision on the color for a new entryway carpet. The choice was between Serenity or Imperial. "Which do you think we chose?" a visitor was asked. "Obviously Serenity," he replied. "No, we chose Imperial," she explained. "You have to break out of the mold sometimes!"

Visitation Retreat Center
3200 SW Dash Point Rd.
Federal Way, WA 98023
(206) 838-9944

Accommodations: *40 rooms for women in singles with half-baths; home-cooked meals in pleasant dining room looking out to gardens and Puget Sound; prayer 5 times daily (3 sung); 25 acres of gardens leading down to beach and bay; closed August and December, plus Easter and holiday weekends; suggested offering: $25 a day.*

Directions: *From Seattle take I-5 South to Exit 143 (Federal Way exit) and drive west on 320th St. to 47th Ave. SW. Continue on 47th to Dash Point Rd. and turn right for 1 mile, watching for sign on left.*

Westminster Abbey
Mission, BC

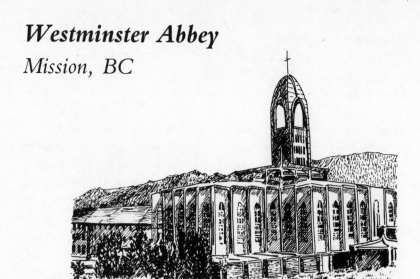

The abbey buildings are on a bluff 400 feet above the Fraser River looking across a wide valley of neat farm fields that end abruptly at wooded foothills that roll like waves to the dazzling snow-capped peaks of the Canadian Coast Mountains. The Benedictine monks came to British Columbia from Mount Angel, Oregon (see page 158) in 1939 at the invitation of the local bishop to establish a monastic presence and found a seminary. When they described their land needs to a realtor, he reacted by saying, "You're looking for heaven on earth!" Undeterred, they kept the memory of the beautiful monastery setting in Oregon before them. The site was eventually found by four priests who got lost exploring back roads. The incident was later described by the abbot in a letter: "We were lead *blindly* to a spot where we believe God wishes our new monastery to be erected. I am trying to contain my feelings but I must admit . . . we were so over-whelmed with the beauty that we fell to our knees to thank God. . . . We knelt and buried a medal of St. Benedict and said the Pater Noster, Thy will be done on earth as it is in heaven. We had absolutely no knowledge of the territory; it seemed like an unseen hand guided us. We rose from our prayers with the comforting thought that we had been led here and God would see to the rest."

The guesthouse, completed in 1971, has 38 rooms and welcomes visitors of all faiths. The rooms are comfortable and convenient to the magnificent church, which has stained-glass windows around a central altar. Here the 35 to 40 monks sing the liturgy four times a day: 5:15 morning praise, mass at 6:30 A.M., midday prayers at 11:50 A.M., and Vespers at 5:30 P.M. The Sunday schedule is slightly different. Meals are served buffet-style in the dining room of a nearby building.

Groups and individuals searching for an atmosphere of silence and the spirit of prayer come regularly. A Lutheran church from a nearby Washington town has held an annual retreat here for almost 20 years. There are no formal programs, but a monk is available for discussion on request.

The Benedictine way has an ecumenical significance tracing back to the 6th century, when St. Benedict founded Monte Cassino in Italy and wrote the famous Rules that are now published in more than 100 languages. For Benedict and his monks, the way to God was through community: "Let us forget ourselves in the common life, forget ourselves in our work, in the liturgy and office; all are an offering back to the Creator from whom all life, goods, and actions have come."

Westminster Abbey
34224 Dewdney Trunk Rd.
Mission, BC V2V 4J2
Canada
(604) 826-8975

Accommodations: *38 rooms (26 singles, 12 doubles) with private washrooms for adults and sometimes families; meals in guest dining room served family-style for small groups and buffet for larger numbers; prayer 4 times daily plus mass in stunning abbey church; 195 acres of beautiful hills, valleys, and vistas; closed July; check with guestmaster for suggested offering and reservations.*

Directions: *1½ hours east of Vancouver. Take BC 1 to Abbottsford exit. Follow BC 11 to Hwy. 7 and turn left at sign on Stave Lake St. Follow signs to abbey on Dewdney Trunk Rd. (turn is across street from Mission Church).*

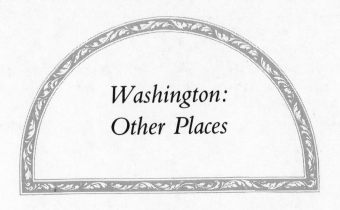

Washington: Other Places

Washington Buddhavanaram, 4401 S. 360th St., **Auburn,** WA 98001. (206) 927-5408

Christ Lutheran Retreat Center, NE 3701 N. Shore Rd., **Belfair,** WA 98528. (206) 275-3354

St. Thomas Center, 14500 Juanita Dr. NE, **Bothell,** WA 98011. (206) 823-1300

Camp Don Bosco, 1401 327th Ave. NE, **Carnation,** WA 98014. (206) 382-4562

Bethlehem Farm, 508 Coal Creek Rd., **Chehalis,** WA 98532. (206) 748-1236

St. Peter the Apostle Retreat Center, 15880 Summit View Rd., **Cowiche,** WA 98923. (509) 678-4935

Soli-time Retreats, 3531 108th St. SE, **Everett,** WA 98208.

Dhiravamsa Foundation, 1660 Word Rd., **Friday Harbor,** WA 98250. (206) 378-5787

Huston Camp and Conference Center, P.O. Box 140, **Gold Bar,** WA 98251. (206) 793-0441

Loma Center for Renewal, 3607 228th Ave. SE, **Issaquah,** WA 98027. (206) 392-1871

St. Placid's Priory Spirituality Center, 500 College St. NE, **Lacey,** WA 98506. (206) 438-1771

Camp Field Retreat Center, P.O. Box 128, **Leavenworth,** WA 98826. (509) 548-7933

Rainbow Lodge, P.O. Box 963, **North Bend,** WA 98045. (206) 888-4181

Seabeck Christian Conference Center, P.O. Box 117, **Seabeck,** WA 98380. (206) 830-5010

Northwest Vipassana Association, 3022 Simmons Rd. NW, **Olympia,** WA 98502. (206) 866-8176

Bodhi Creek Farm Retreat Center, 7601 Kendall Rd., **Sumas,** WA 98295. (206) 599-2106

St. Mary's Conference and Retreat Center, 107 Spencer Rd., **Toledo,** WA 98591. (206) 864-6464

St. Andrew's House, 87550 Hwy. 106, **Union,** WA 98592. (206) 898-2362

Burton Camp and Conference Center, 9326 SW Bayview Dr., **Vashon Island,** WA 98070. (206) 622-3935

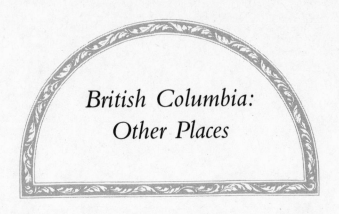

British Columbia: Other Places

Kagyu Kunkhyab Chuling, 4939 Sidley St., **Burnaby,** BC V5J 1T6, Canada. (604) 434-4920

Prince of Peace Priory, 2904 Josephine St., Box 960, **Chemainus,** BC V0R 1K0, Canada. (604) 246-9578

Hollyhock, Box 127, Manson's Landing, **Cortes Island,** BC V0P 1K0, Canada. (604) 935-6465

Mount St. Nicholas Priory, 4655 Westside Rd., **Kamloops,** BC V2C 1Z3, Canada. (604) 579-9150

Seton House of Prayer, RR 4 Site 20 Box 9, **Kelowna,** BC V1Y 7R3, Canada. (604) 764-4333

Yasodhara Ashram, P.O. Box 9A, **Kootenay Bay,** BC V0B 1X0, Canada. (604) 227-9224

Anawim House of Prayer, Bealby Point, **Nelson,** BC V1L 1T4, Canada. (604) 352-2930

Sorrento Centre, Box 99, **Sorrento,** BC V0E 2W0, Canada. (604) 675-2421

Queenswood, 2494 Arbutus Rd., **Victoria,** BC V8N 1V8, Canada. (604) 477-3822

Glossary

Ango An intensive 90-day training period in the Zen Buddhist tradition. A Japanese word meaning "peaceful dwelling."

Canonical hours The liturgy of the hours is the official daily prayer cycle of the Catholic church, an adaptation of the liturgy of the synagogue, which has evolved over the centuries. The "hours" consist of Vigils, Lauds, Terce, Sext, None, Vespers, and Compline. "Seven times a day do I praise thee . . ." (Psalms 119:164).

Centering prayer Meditative prayer, using a sacred word to focus attention internally. Father Thomas Keating's book *Open Mind, Open Heart* describes this in detail.

Charismatic retreat Christian healing retreat involving prophecy and praying in tongues.

Cursillo An uplifting weekend retreat for groups to experience their religion from a new perspective.

Deacon A cleric ranking below a priest.

Directed retreat Usually a six-to-eight-day period of silent prayer that includes a daily meeting with a spiritual director.

Divine office Official, formal, liturgical prayer of the Church.

Engaged encounter Weekend retreat sponsored by the Church for engaged couples (or marriage encounters for married couples) to explore and clarify their belief systems and values.

Enneagram An ancient circular diagram that can be used to bring insight into the divine activity within each person.

Foundation A branch of the main monastery.

Grand (Great) Silence A period of silence usually following evening prayer until after breakfast the following day.

Guided retreat Retreat that includes meeting with a spiritual director from time to time, but not on a daily basis.

Hermitage A secluded residence.

Mantra A sacred word or group of words whose repetition is conducive to quieting the mind, often used during meditation.

Meyers-Briggs Personality descriptions based on the work of C. G. Jung that have been adapted to discovery-of-self workshops.

Oblate A layperson affiliated with a particular order who adopts a mod-ified vow—a way of deepening lay spirituality. Each order confers certain special privileges on oblates; for example, the Carmelites allow their oblates to be buried in the Carmelite habit.

Poustinia "Silence of God." A designated period or place where a complete retreat, silence, fasting, and separation from normal activities takes place.

Private retreat A time of solitude without guidance or direction.

Refectory Monastery dining hall.

Soto Zen One of two active schools of Zen Buddhism in Japan. Stresses meditation practice as a path to enlightenment. It relies on heart-to-heart transmission, since it has no scripture.

Spiritual director A guide or adviser who helps put your spiritual journey into perspective and connects it to your daily life.

Sufism An eclectic school of mysticism with roots in Islam that has grown to encompass many traditions and includes an elaborate symbolism much used by the poets. There is scholarly disagreement on the exact origins of the name, some saying it comes from a Persian word meaning "wisdom," others that it comes from the word *sūf* (wool) because of the coarse robes early Sufi ascetics and renunciates wore.

T'ai chi ch'uan Chinese "meditation in motion," a series of flowing, gentle movements or exercises intended to quiet the mind and body.

Taizé A small ecumenical monastery in southern France where one of the brothers developed a particular form of chant that has become popular throughout the world.

Vipassana meditation Buddhist "insight" meditation first used by nuns, monks, and laypeople in Southeast Asia to attain a quality of mindfulness and understanding through direct observation of the mind and body. It embraces the belief that loving-kindness, compassion, and a spirit of generosity can be cultivated consciously.

Yurt Originally a circular tent of felt or skins on a framework of poles used by nomads in Mongolia, it has been adapted by others as a dwelling made out of various materials.

With thanks to Chimney Sweep Books in Santa Cruz, CA, for their help on many definitions.

Index

Other Places

About the Authors

Marcia and Jack Kelly are writers who live in New York City. Over the years they have chosen monasteries and retreats as stopping places in their travels. Their first book, *Sanctuaries—The Northeast*, was published in 1991. This book is the second in the series, a result of many happy sojourns. They have also edited *One Hundred Graces*, a collection of mealtime graces, gathered along the way.

Other

Bell Tower Books

The pure sound of the bell summons us into the present moment. The timeless ring of truth is expressed in many different voices, each one magnifying and illuminating the sacred. The clarity of its song resonates within us and calls us away from those things that often distract us—that which was, that which might be—to That Which Is.

Being Home: *A Book of Meditations*
by Gunilla Norris
Photographs by Greta D. Sibley

An exquisite modern book of hours, a celebration of mindfulness in everyday activities.

0-517-58159-0 hardcover, 1991

Nourishing Wisdom: *A New Understanding of Eating*
by Marc David

A practical way out of dietary confusion, a book that advocates awareness in eating and reveals how our attitude to food reflects our attitude to life.

0-517-57636-8 hardcover, 1991

Sanctuaries—The Northeast: *A Guide to Lodgings in Monasteries, Abbeys, and Retreats of the United States*
by Jack and Marcia Kelly

The first in a series of regional guides for those in search of renewal and a little peace.

0-517-57727-5 paperback, 1991

Grace Unfolding: *Psychotherapy in the Spirit of the Tao-te ching*
by Greg Johanson and Ron Kurtz

The interaction of client and therapist illuminated through the gentle power and wisdom of Lao Tzu's ancient Chinese classic.

0-517-58449-2 hardcover, 1991

Self-Reliance
The Wisdom of Ralph Waldo Emerson as Inspiration for Daily Living
Selected and with an introduction by Richard Whelan

A distillation of Emerson's essential spiritual writings for contemporary readers.

0-517-58512-X paperback, 1991

Compassion in Action: *Setting Out on the Path of Service*
by Ram Dass and Mirabai Bush

Heartfelt encouragement and advice for those ready to commit time and energy to relieving suffering in the world.

0-517-57635-X paperback, 1992

Letters from a Wild State: *Rediscovering Our True Relationship to Nature*
by James G. Cowan

A luminous interpretation of Aboriginal spiritual experience applied to the leading issue of our time: the care of the earth.

0-517-58770-X hardcover, 1992

Silence, Simplicity, and Solitude: *A Guide for Spiritual Retreat*
by David A. Cooper

This classic guide will be required reading for anyone contemplating a retreat.

0-517-58620-7 hardcover, 1992

One Hundred Graces
Selected by Marcia and Jack Kelly
With calligraphy by Christopher Gausby

A collection of mealtime graces from many traditions, beautifully inscribed in calligraphy reminiscent of the manuscripts of medieval Europe.

0-517-58567-7 hardcover, 1992

The Heart of Stillness: *The Elements of Spiritual Practice*
by David A. Cooper

How to deal with the difficulties that can arise in meditation, both on retreat and at home—a companion volume to *Silence, Simplicity, and Solitude.*

0-517-58621-5 hardcover, 1992

Bell Tower books are for sale at your local bookstore or you may call 1-800-733-3000 to order with a credit card.